INSTANTLY STOP PROCRASTINATION

4 Powerful Concepts That Will Help You Effectively
Complete the Tasks You Keep Avoiding

by

Patrick Drechsler

Table of Contents

Introduction

You have a task to perform, but everything in you goes on strike at the thought of doing it; even though you know that if you don't do it, there will be negative consequences. Sound familiar?

Is it your term paper at university perhaps?

Or rather that project at work that has been bugging you for ages?

You already know how putting it off ends – with numerous cups of coffee and some extremely late nights. And yet, you still you do it – You procrastinate!

But what exactly is procrastination?

The word procrastination has its roots in Latin and originally described a *positive quality*. This would suggest that procrastinating isn't necessarily a fault on your part but could just as well be an indication that the task itself is redundant. Procrastination doesn't need to be branded as *negative* without first looking more closely at it. And that's what this guidebook aims to do. The methods highlighted in this book will show you how to prevent procrastination, and eventually how to completely remove the tendency altogether.

But how is it possible to prevent procrastination, when some tasks are such a nuisance that everything in your being refuses to complete them?

Personal transformation sometimes occurs from one day to the next when people have drastic experiences; like the death of a loved one, the end of a relationship, or a big fall after previous success – these types of situations can cause people to have the much-cited *now-first-right attitude*, where a loved one's character is fundamentally changed in order to save his relationship; or when every ounce of someone's strength is mobilized to find a way back to success. The brain researcher Gerhard Roth calls these events *teachable moments*.

Teachable moments usually release previously unimagined forces. The problem though, is that people can end up handling themselves destructively. The associated, *tunnel vision* can lead people to neglect their own well-being in order to achieve their goal. This occurs with most forms of rapid change, that tend not to be sustainable in the long run. But what can still be learned from them, is that if certain events can transform a person quickly, then change *is* indeed possible.

The path laid out in this book is not a *teachable moment* and does not claim to be a *quick cure*. Instead, it offers you methods that lead to a *sustainable* way out of procrastination, acting *without* tunnel vision and *with* consideration for your health.

In chapter 1, we explore different ways to assess procrastination, as well as the most common causes for it. Once these causes are known, there are several self-tests and methods that are tailored to your unique tendencies. Think of it like a customer service site, where you can scroll through numerous options and find the ones most helpful to you.

If you tend to struggle with motivation for example, the second chapter provides useful insights to help you deal with it. While chapters 3, 4, and 5, go into a deeper analysis of the causes of procrastination, with practical exercises that will help you to deal with it effectively. Including showing you how to develop more self-conviction and greater self-control; how to set priorities, and how to slow down, in today's fast-paced, digital world.

You *can* change. You have already taken the first big step by selecting this book – it is an excellent place to start! The next step will be to read it thoroughly and put into practice what you learn. You don't have to change anything big overnight or throw your worldviews out of the window. Everything we will show you, will always be just a small and manageable step, that leads you to a sustainable path that will be your long-awaited key to success, in the fight against procrastination.

On the trail of procrastination

As we have already learned, procrastination can actually be helpful as an indication that you could benefit from rearranging some aspects of your life. It can help you to understand when to let go of things, relationships, and tasks that no longer add value to you.

There are different interpretations for the cause of procrastination. For example, you may be a very disciplined and consistent person who has simply imposed too many tasks on himself. In this case, either prioritizing, or even abandoning certain tasks altogether, could be the right solution for you.

If you are a person who is easily distracted by impulses, due to the fast pace of life associated with digital media, Concepts 3 and 4 will offer you concrete approaches to solve this problem.

First though, we will look at the different, scientifically defined, types of procrastination that led us to create the concepts and tasks in this book. The goal being, to show you how procrastination can be used as an important decision-making tool. A tool that has become increasingly established in recent decades through digitization.

In search of causes – latest findings and old theories

Recent findings have shown that some of the general tendencies that cause procrastination, are perfectionism, rebellious behavior, and a pronounced interest in new things. With perfectionism, the cause is the desire to perform a task to the highest standard while at the same time lacking the knowledge to do so, leading instead to postponement. Rebellious behavior and a strong interest in new things are equally easy to understand. But these findings don't go into the same depth as we will in the upcoming pages, beginning with the 4 causes of procrastination described below.

Cause 1: Aversion to the task

Task aversion is a classic cause of procrastination according to numerous studies. Aversion can often result from a lack of ability. If a person is unable to perform a task well, procrastination may occur. In addition to lack of skills, matching with personal interests is also a relevant factor: A person has the ability to perform a task, but still doesn't, because it doesn't interest him. This can result in underachievement, which leads to procrastination.

Aversion is often determined by a person's individual character and corresponding tendencies towards motivation. Some people are able to motivate themselves right away even to the tasks they feel a great aversion to. Other people need time to motivate themselves or they just do not succeed at all. *How* and to what extent you can motivate yourself varies with each person. But developing motivation is a skill that can be learned through training. After all, motivation means nothing more than finding motives.

According to Steel (2012), researchers have determined that rewards for performing unwanted tasks are good motivational factors. The closer the reward, the more the willingness to pursue the task increases. There are several other methods too, that we will highlight in the further chapters of this book.

Self-test questions to help you find the right concept for you:

> ➤ Having a hard time getting started with the task in the first place? Concept 1 offers the appropriate ways to tackle this problem.
> ➤ Don't know where to start because there are too many tasks? It's worth taking a look at both Concepts 1 and 4.
> ➤ Feeling overwhelmed by the task and therefore reject it? All of the concepts offer you potential solutions, but especially 1, 2 and 4.

Cause 2: Lack of conviction that you can succeed

Success, in one form or another, is a component of life that every person strives for. To achieve it, challenges must be met effectively. In some cases, great effort is required, and in other cases, less so. The less the effort and the greater the success, the less the tendency to procrastinate. The greater the effort and the less the success, the greater the tendency to procrastinate. Great effort often requires even greater motivation.

People who have confidence in themselves are likely to cope better than a person who is not convinced that he or she will succeed. Lack of conviction is also referred to as low self-efficacy.

The term self-efficacy refers to a person's ability to successfully overcome challenges.

Who has high self-efficacy? As a general rule, people who have already mastered several crises can be said to have high self-efficacy. In addition to this general form of self-efficacy, there is also specific self-efficacy, where individuals are convinced of their success in specific areas.

Example

You're sure to have fond memories of your favorite subjects when you were at school. In those subjects, in which you got good grades, or which you enjoyed more, you were more likely to succeed. This probably meant that you were convinced of your success, right?

You understand the basic principle: conviction is a great motivator. Not surprisingly, the keyword *motivation* comes up again. Conviction can be compared to an insurance policy or a binding contract. You are absolutely convinced in your mind that you will succeed in performing a task, so you feel a bit like you have signed a contract that assures you of success. Would you perform the task if success were certain? Perhaps not if the success did not justify the effort, but otherwise, certainty increases motivation. Even though there is no such thing as 100 percent certainty, the added value of great conviction cannot be denied, because it suggests certainty to your subconscious.

Self-test questions to help you find the right concept:

➤ You doubt it is possible for you to accomplish the task well? Concept 2 and partly Concept 3 are tailored for you!

8

> ➢ Your determination is not great because you don't really care about the task? In this case, you should deal with Concept 4 first and foremost.

> ➢ You prefer to devote yourself to other things because they are more promising or fulfilling? Look especially into Concept 3!

Cause 3: Low self-control, high impulsivity

Impulsivity and lack of self-control are often associated with outbursts of anger, acts of violence, or other highly conspicuous acts. However, drastic reactions aren't always the result of these traits.

In the case of procrastination, people who cannot control themselves well tend to procrastinate. Lack of self-control has several possible causes:

> ➢ Habit: Habits are automated behavioral patterns programmed into the human brain. The inclination is stored in the subconscious, making it difficult to resist acting in the same way. As a result, people regularly give in to their habits. The more pronounced the habit, the more difficult it is to control oneself and resist the temptation.

> ➢ Character: People all have their own specific character traits, including impulsivity. Impulsivity can develop at any stage in life for various reasons. For example, growing up with parents who tend to use a loud tone, bad career choices, meddling life partners and drastic experiences can all be potential triggers for impulsivity, as they become ingrained in a person's character. Affected individuals find

it difficult to distance themselves emotionally from an issue, often giving free rein to their emotions.

➤ Disease: Individuals with certain mental illnesses, either
congenital or developed over the course of life, often tend
to be impulsive. Impulsivity due to lack of emotional control is a borderline mental illness. An example of a mental
illness in which impulsivity may result not from emotions
but from the very nature of the disorder is ADHD.

These 3 triggers are frequent causes of behavioral patterns
that develop into a tendency to procrastinate. A lack of self-control alone is not usually enough. But combined with a general dislike of the task and low self-efficacy, you have all the ingredients
for procrastination. Then counterproductive emotions arise that
encourage giving in and prevent the task from being performed.

An interesting insight: Motivation beats emotion! Should you
associate more with low self-control, then you may feel consoled
by the fact that you can usually beat this by treating the first 2
causes. Because if you positively influence your motivation levels
to such an extent that you believe you will succeed in the exercise
and feel motivated to perform the task, you will be better able to
defy the impulses that encourage you to procrastinate.

Self-test questions to help you find the right concept:

➤ You give in to various impulses that distract you while
performing the task? Concept 3 is tailor-made for you.
While concept 2 also offers indirect good advice and
methods too.

➤ You often get distracted by other things which affects
your consistency in performing a task? Concept 4 helps

you to weigh between several perspectives to deal with this issue.

> You are generally always full of energy and switch back and forth between different things? In this case, we recommend studying Concepts 3 and 4.

Cause 4: Long time horizon

Imagine a task that you are facing that you keep putting off. Maybe you currently have such a task that you are working on... if not, then just think of one. Now imagine that you have to do it for only 5 minutes for it to be completely finished, with the success safely in your pocket. Would you say no to this deal? Probably not.

Now imagine you had to do the same task for 5 minutes every day for 3 weeks. Here it already becomes more difficult. Then think that you have to do it for several hours a week for several years. An unpleasant shiver is likely to run down your spine at the thought of it in this case.

The longer the time horizon associated with a task, the higher the risk that the task will be postponed. This is doubly treacherous. Because in addition to the problems caused by the postponement itself, unforeseeable events in the future are also a potential cause for postponement.

Self-test questions to help you find the right Concept:

> You always devote yourself to your tasks in a relaxed and leisurely manner?

Take a look at Concept 1 and see if it wouldn't be better with a little more consistency and determination.

➢ Other people distract you from the task at hand and you always refer to the long time-horizon you still have? Learn more about this in Concepts 2 and 3.

➢ Because of the long time-horizon, would you rather perform the many other tasks that are in front of you that are more urgent?

In Concept 4, learn whether it would not be better to think about fixed prioritizations and a reduction of tasks.

Determining the usefulness of a task – is procrastination appropriate?

Apart from the causes, there are other forces at work that lead to procrastination. According to Dr. Steel (2007), the following influencing factors are also present: Expectations of the task, value of the task, and delay. Using these influencing factors, Dr. Steel created the Temporal Motivation Theory to determine the utility of a task.

$$Usefullness = \frac{E \times V}{D}$$

As interesting as it may be to have a concrete formula for calculating the probability of procrastination, it should be just as clear at the same time that no concrete numbers can be used for all the influencing factors, which is why the result cannot be concrete either. Certainly, models could be created according to which the numbers for expectations, appreciation, procrastination and finally benefit could be derived by a question-answer game with fixed values for each answer. But the model would hardly be suitable for general use.

What you take from this formula in the ideal case is only the connections between these influencing factors. Now it is possible for you to anticipate the possible extent of your procrastination in order to use the measures described in the concepts of this book to improve over time.

But what exactly are the relationships that this model describes?

➤ Expectations: Expectations represent the probability you expect to get a certain result. Negative expectations are basically nothing more than low self-efficacy (see causes). If expectations are low, a low number would be put into the formula.

➤ Value: The value of a task or your appreciation of it is measured by your perception of how rewarding the performance of the task is. A high learning factor that would be valued would result in a high propensity to perform the task. The number in the formula would be high. If the value placed on the task was low (see aversion to the task under causes), the number entered in the formula would be low.

➤ Delay: How much you delay a task also affects its usefulness. It makes sense to include this value in the fraction of the formula in the denominator, because otherwise the formula would not make sense; examples will follow shortly.

> ➤ Benefit: The usefulness of the task is representative of the likelihood of procrastination. This is based on the idea that useful tasks are not postponed. If procrastination does occur, it is only for valid reasons. In general, tasks with a high utility do not have a tendency to procrastination. A low benefit, on the other hand, leads to an increased probability of procrastination.

Three examples are used to calculate the benefit. For the formula, it is assumed that scales from 1 to 10 are used. This is practical in that the results are then percentages and allow a quick overall assessment of the task. The numbers in the examples are subjective estimates. You would also calculate with such estimates if you want to use the formula.

Example 1

Hannes F. has very low expectations about the output of a task, but a high appreciation towards the execution, because it makes him repeat and consolidate existing knowledge. He pursues the task without delay. The formula could look like this:

$$Uselfullness = \frac{2 \times 8}{1}$$

$$Usefullness = \frac{16}{1}$$

$$Usefullness = 16 \ (16\,\%)$$

Example 2

Ina L. expects the greatest profit from the task and likes to do it because she enjoys it. She does not delay the task, but always performs it at the scheduled time. This is how the potential formula is created:

$$Usefullness = \frac{10 \times 9}{1}$$

$$Usefullness = \frac{90}{1}$$

$$Usefullness = 90 \ (90 \ \%)$$

Example 3

Thomas G. has devastatingly low expectations and no appreciation for the task. Discipline is also non-existent in Thomas, which is why he delays the task as long as possible. The formula in this extreme case would be as follows:

$$Usefullness = \frac{E \times V}{D}$$

$$Uselfullness = \frac{1 \times 1}{10}$$

$$Usefullness = \frac{1}{10} \ (0,1 \ \%!)$$

As we can see, the formula is very well thought out. The delay in the denominator of the fraction ensures that high or low delays have the desired effects on the result. A high delay minimizes the overall result and invalidates good intermediate results from the numerator at the top of the fraction (E x V), a low delay does just the opposite. The benefit, when calculating on a scale of 1 to 10 for the 3 influencing factors that present themselves, takes 100 as the highest value and 1/10 as the lowest value. Thus, the result can simply be represented as a percentage.

Low benefit encourages questioning

Even without calculating in this form using concrete numbers from a scale, it is helpful to keep the formula in mind. This is because it shows how different influencing factors are interrelated. If you take into account several components that define the value of an influencing factor, this formula provides you with a good decision-making aid to know whether you should pursue the task or activity at all.

Let's assume that the benefit would be so low that it would be less than 10 percent. This would be an almost damning verdict for the task in question. The best example is an obligation in an association, which you pursue: After some time, you notice that this association is rather disorganized. The work does not reach the planned effect by far. Moreover, it is not unlikely that the goals will be missed year after year. You understandably have lower and lower expectations of the task, and feel no appreciation during the execution, because the association hardly lives up to its purpose, so you procrastinate longer and longer on your tasks as a result. In this case, the situation is clear: resign from the association. Find a better club elsewhere, where you can better develop motivation. In this example, procrastination is not a negative thing, but an important decision-making tool. Even the most disciplined people would break with the club in a case like this; unless they had the chance to turn the club around themselves and push it forward according to their own ideas. But these are rare exceptions.

The formula for calculating the benefit can also be applied to interpersonal relationships and professions. Basically, it can be applied to all areas in which you have to make a decision, and then fulfill obligations.

Explanation based on interpersonal relationships

Now, when it comes to interpersonal relationships, *usefulness* isn't necessarily appropriate. After all, friends, life partners or even acquaintances are not there to be of use to you. In fact, it is a term that seems out of place given the emotional connection we have to these people. Feel free to replace the term with *attachment* if you like. Probably you have experienced two people drifting apart. They may develop conflicting interests or pursue different careers. The mutual benefits of the relationship to each other or the bond between them starts to diminish.

> ➤ Expectations: Expectations can also be reduced between two people. Initially, partner A still has the hope that partner B will someday remember his birthday or their wedding anniversary. In the beginning, girlfriend C has the hope that she will be able to help boyfriend D out of a drug quagmire. When these hopes give way to disappointments, expectations fall. As expectations fall, the added value of a relationship falls too.

> ➤ Appreciation: In the beginning, many things are new in a relationship. Almost everything that the significant other has to offer is fascinating – from playing the piano beautifully to having an attractive body to having money in the

bank account (people have different incentives to feel appreciation). The special value of these things is often reduced over the course of the relationship and the appreciation may be lost.

➤ Procrastination: In relationships, when the delay in performing favors or duties for the other person increases, this type of procrastination suggests a diminished sense of care has developed. It starts with the simplest things, such as when a partner complies with his or her partner's request to wash the dishes or take out the trash less and less often...

Procrastination is also noticeable in interpersonal relationships. It is one of the factors that provides insight into the value of a relationship. Nevertheless, it must be taken into account that, in addition to the 3 influencing factors from the formula, emotions are at work. These emotions make you think back to the past or develop optimism for the future. The recommendation is therefore that you use this formula in relationships as a decision-making aid by taking into account the strength of the emotions. If you feel emotionally attached, do not break with the person, but look for ways to raise expectations, appreciation and benefits, while reducing the delays.

In the case of negative emotions, combined with a low calculated benefit from the formula, it is indeed worth considering whether the relationship should not be paused or ended. What reasons do you think there could be for friends to go their separate ways, for married couples to split up, and for newcomers to get tired of talking to their neighbors after just 2 weeks? The formula offers some sound solutions.

Example based on profession

Talking about a low amount of benefit for your profession is a sensitive topic. Because it could make you realize that it's time to change professions altogether. But who can simply afford to change professions?

Expectations of and appreciation for a profession are largely derived from previous experience, prospects in the industry, and the careers of one's colleagues. The better all these factors are, the higher the expectations. Esteem is a very important factor because it is largely what tends to keep most employees, and self-employed people in their jobs. A large proportion of people have no prospect of changing jobs just like that. It would often involve too much effort because retraining would have to be done in addition to the current job. This effort can often be enough that it makes people feel like changing jobs is virtually impossible. Therefore, most people have a distinct appreciation towards their jobs. After all, it brings them money, which they need to live. So, it is hardly surprising that even people who haven't completely liked their job for decades, do not change it. With regards to career, delays are a very important signal. Because even a person who has despised his job for decades will, if he has no alternative to earn money, usually complete tasks without delay. This is because automatisms and routines take hold that are stronger than low motivation levels. In turn, people who procrastinate with work usually do so because they are not completely dependent on the job. After all, who would take the risk of not adequately fulfilling their duty, of being fired, and of being left without an income? As a rule, only a person who has alternative jobs available. Of course, there are even exceptions to this as well...

The example of profession illustrates how closely lack of appreciation and procrastination are linked. There is no denying that procrastination in this case should always be the trigger for serious reflection: Am I still right in this job? What prospects do I have to change the job? And above all: What are the existing problems, and can they be resolved within the profession or with the respective employer? In the most extreme case, it is indeed advisable to think about quitting. After all, low esteem and postponement of duties lead to deteriorated work performance, which in the long run will most likely lead to consequences initiated by the employer anyway.

Honesty with yourself

Now for some general hints about the thematized *Temporal Motivation Theory*. The whole formula can only be of help if you are honest with yourself. A common mistake people tend make is to reject personal responsibility. If you have agreed with your partner to improve on a certain point and do not do so, you will not be able to say that the relationship is failing because of your partner.

Example

If the garbage is left lying around everywhere and the willingness to clean up decreases with the duration of the relationship, then the relationship will most likely fail because of you. Meanwhile, the likelihood of finding a new partner with a penchant for clutter and mess is slim. Here it is necessary to take a look at your own behavior.

When discussing whether procrastination is a long overdue sign of a necessary change or a personal weakness that you need to work on, being honest with yourself is an incredibly important component. Impulsive people in particular don't find it easy to blame themselves. They let emotions and impulses control them and often disregard rational judgments. With some distance from the event, however, even impulsive people will succeed in putting their emotions aside and being honest with themselves.

But how do I become honest with myself? How do I manage to make an objective judgment about whether procrastination is a sign of necessary change or a mistake on my part?

Self-reflection is the key. This requires that you take time in the evenings for reviewing your days, so you can deal with how you felt and decide whether you did everything right. Evenings are perfect for this, once everything has settled down and the day is over, it is optimal for self-reflection. Ideally, you would write down your feelings so that you can still understand them several days later and do not forget them again. Self-reflection should be done without emotional attachment, if possible. Take a differentiated look at the facts from several perspectives to decide whether you did the right thing.

Task 1

Take some time each evening for a week to think deeply about your procrastination. As you do so, consider whether you might have overlooked several positive aspects of the task at hand. Write down all the positive and negative aspects. Collect it over several evenings and then see if anything has changed in your expectations, appreciation, usefulness, and urge to procrastinate. You may be more motivated to pursue the activity because you see a greater benefit in it.

Self-reflection sometimes works more, sometimes less well. Practice makes perfect. Here are some useful further methods to help you find out the reason for your procrastination:

> Use personal examples: Personal examples are especially advantageous in a professional context. If you suspect low career prospects, it makes sense to find out about people in your company or in the industry in general. If it turns out that, with a lot of effort and dedication, a considerable climb up the career ladder is possible after all, you will gain greater expectations of the profession and a higher appreciation for it. You will realize that the problem was not a lack of prospects, but your lack of knowledge. Personal examples can be used in all types of tasks to develop motivation. You can even use them in sports by looking at pictures or YouTube videos of role models. Surely you can find one or the other person who started an activity under the same (adverse) circumstances as you and still became successful.

> Have conversations: As soon as you have conversations about your situation, you will gain additional perspectives. You are probably familiar with the recommendation that certain changes or challenges should be tackled in pairs, because then you can motivate each other. Conversations have the same intention. If you present your problem, you will get helpful information from other people, which will give you new perspectives on your prospects and increase your appreciation. You'll also get tips against procrastination here and there from other people. Conversations are worthwhile. A little tip, if you're uncomfortable admitting

that the problem affects you: talk about the problem as if someone else had it. If you tell them that a friend is in the same situation, it will be easier for you to talk openly about the issue.

➤ <u>Turn the tables:</u> Turn the tables by imagining what it would take for you to always follow through on the task in a timely manner. What would have to happen for your expectations and appreciation of the task to be so high that you would no longer put it off? Even imagine absurd scenarios, but stay within a realistic framework. You may end up realizing that what should be possible is already there, but you have ignored it so far. And maybe, in addition, much of what you want is possible, provided you put a little effort into the task. In extreme cases, you may realize that no prerequisites in the world could increase your affection towards the task. If it gets to that point, then it's a sign that the procrastination is just a logical consequence of your profound dislike for a task, and you should abandon the task as soon as possible and find something new.

Task 2

Now devote yourself to the methods described. During the day, before you do the self-reflection, do one of the 3 methods. Take one day for each of them. Of course, it doesn't have to be the entire day. Methods like turning the tables may only require 30 minutes of time, while conversations require finding several people first and then having the conversations. The fact is that the 3 methods presented will enrich your self-reflection and you will gain new insights through the methods themselves.

Sometimes the causes lie with yourself. In particular, if you look at your past experiences in life, you will discover clues as to whether the task is generally bad or if you just need to work on yourself. Honesty is the basis for a reasonable analysis. **Remember**: No relationship will end, no job will be quit, and no task will be simply discarded, without a completely honest analysis of what the reason for procrastination is, whether it is justified and how you can defuse it, if necessary, by changing your perspective!

"Procrastinare!" – Procrastination through the ages

The negative stigma associated with the word *procrastination* today did not exist in the past. Although it was a long time ago, the original view proves helpful as a support for you to determine in which situations procrastination is beneficial for you.

Did you know?

The word *procrastination* has its origin in Latin, namely in the verb *procrastinare*. Surprisingly, the original meaning of this word is not negative. In the past, putting something off and thus waiting until the next day was considered a sign of wisdom, and testified to good thinking. It is not known how the word came to have the negative meaning it has today.

Procrastination used to be seen as a positive approach. Today, on the other hand, it is perceived negatively. How could it come to this? Possible answers are provided by the documentary *Zeit ist Geld* (2016), which was shown on the German TV channel *arte*. As the title suggests, the plot focuses on time. Although procrastination is not the main topic of the documentary, it does come up. In fact, there is a close connection between procrastination, time and – in a more distant sense, which will be explained in a moment – money. Time defines procrastination. If there were no time, nothing could be put off. As a deepening aspect, you have learned that a long time-horizon for unwanted tasks increases the probability of procrastination.

How does money fit into this context? What does money stand for anyway?

Acceleration in today's world causes problems

The scope for interpretation is wide, but in the documentary it is mainly attributed to capitalism and globalization. In addition, digitization as an influencing factor must not be disregarded. Anyone who follows the history of time, especially since capitalism's inception, learns that the first punch clocks came in during the course of industrialization. Work has been measurable since that time at the earliest. Words like *productivity* and *optimization* crept into factory jargon, that of companies and even private individuals. In the early 20th century, universal time was established in Paris. Time was measurable everywhere. Looking further into the future, we notice its influence with digitalization that was supposed to create more simplicity and freedom. But that's still not the case in the reality of companies today. Instead of digital possibilities loosening the lines for employees, expectations are increased. Digitalization is not bypassing private households either. In general, the new possibilities serve only to tempt people to be more productive. It is becoming increasingly out of fashion to slow down. The documentary asks the question:

"Where do you find the time for relaxation and idleness when any time outside of work is considered a lost minute?"

25

Career. Prospects. Optimization through digitization. Social trends. All these things tempt people to take on many obligations. Maybe there are even so many obligations that it can only go well for a limited period of time in the first place? This is a question you can ask yourself: Are you allowing yourself enough time off or are you overwhelming yourself with the amount of tasks? If the latter were the case, then procrastination wouldn't even begin to be surprising. It would be a logical consequence of being over-whelmed.

Most·people have a guilty conscience when they put some-thing off until the next day. Whether this guilty conscience is jus-tified must be judged in relation to the overall burden. In today's times, it seems more important than ever to set priorities. Not being able to say *no* to individual tasks or activities can become a huge problem over time. Concept 4 will help you with these things with a wealth of exercises and the ultimate guide to prioritization.

Deceleration counteracts procrastination

Surprisingly, over the last few decades, as technological pro-gress has been at its highest, the amount of mental illness has also been increasing. An interesting change within the German popu-lation can be observed compared to the early 2000s: Back then, it was the unemployed who had a disproportionate incidence of mental illness. Today, it is the employed. Sick leave due to mental illness has risen steadily in this country since 2006. Cases of inca-pacity to work increased by 50% from 2006 to 2016, and the amount of days of incapacity to work has increased by 80% over the same period. A deeper look at the statistics reveals that the following mental illnesses led to incapacity to work among employees in 2013:

> Affective disorders (including burnout, gloom, dejection, elevated or irritable mood, persistent mild depressed mood, decreased drive): 46,2 %

> Neurotic, stress and somatoform disorders (including anxiety disorder, panic disorder, obsessive-compulsive disorder, panic attacks): 44.9%.

> Disorders due to the use of substances that affect the psyche: 3.9%.

> Schizophrenia and delusional ideation: 2.2%.

> Personality and behavioral disorders: 1 %

> Other: 1.9 %

Source: Statista

According to information from the *Ärzteblatt*, the proportion of early retirements in 2010 was 36%. More than one third of German pensioners thus retired earlier than actually planned! The BKK Health Report of 2018 also identifies drastic increases in mental illnesses within the past 40 years.

Did you know?

In Japan, burnout affected 40% of the population in the 1980s. As a major global power at the time, the country slid into an economic crisis because – almost unbelievably – the population worked too much without taking vacations. As a result, there was hardly any consumption among the population, which is why a recession occurred.

What do mental illnesses have to do with procrastination?

Many things. First of all, it should be noted that mental illness promotes procrastination. Those who are listless, depressed, or in otherwise poor mental health will have a greater tendency to put off tasks. In these cases, the cause of procrastination is usually the same as the cause of mental illness. You'd be surprised to know how many of the mental illnesses go undetected for a long time or slowly develop. In some circumstances, overwork and increasing procrastination lead to the discovery of the mental illness in the first place. In any case, you need to ask yourself if the procrastination is not caused by an excess of tasks. If you have so many tasks in front of you that you can hardly cope with them and only with the greatest of efforts, you must make changes to your daily routine. Otherwise – and this is absolutely serious – sooner or later you may develop a mental illness.

However, mental illnesses do not only promote procrastination. It is the same the other way around. Imagine that you put off one or more very important things every day. You would then eventually get into a predicament of having to catch up on everything. However, this does not necessarily cause mental illness, which becomes apparent over a longer period of time. It often becomes problematic if you regularly put things off. It can cause you to start doubting yourself at some point. In the worst case, you feel inferior, even though you are not. In addition, other people may put pressure on you and constantly remind you that you have things to do. They may even make fun of you. One domino sets the other one in motion, and so initially simple procrastination turns into a deeper psychological problem.

These explanations are in no way intended to frighten you. They are only meant to illustrate that procrastination is becoming more and more common in today's world. Almost analogous to the increase in mental illness, an increase in the number of things that are put off by different people in different contexts is becoming noticeable. There may or may not be a connection to mental illness. Most people who seek help for procrastination are not affected by mental illness. But life is long. To ensure that everything runs smoothly psychologically and in terms of life plans in the many years to come, it is reasonable to consider whether procrastination might not be the natural consequence of unnecessarily excessive demands. Again, we refer you to Concept 4, which will also help you with this concern.

The most important things in a nutshell

- ➤ Procrastination usually arises from dissatisfaction or excessive demands.
- ➤ Dissatisfaction may arise from a general dislike of an activity, certain impulses related to the activity, a lack of appreciation, or low self-efficacy.
- ➤ Being overwhelmed is a classic consequence of taking on too many tasks. If possible, priorities should be set and rest breaks should be integrated into everyday life. Otherwise, in the worst case, it is even possible for mental illness to manifest itself.
- ➤ If a task, relationship or activity is of little benefit, then its maintenance should be questioned. In this sense, procrastination is a decision-making tool for changes in everyday life.

➢ Whenever a task is a must-do or related to something personally important, procrastination must be addressed.

➢ Likewise, measures against procrastination must be initiated when the smallest and most self-evident things of everyday life, such as hygienic or social norms, are postponed due to procrastination.

Concept 1 | Purely a matter of attitude: Finding the right start

Your attitude describes what opinion you have of something. It is the expectations you have towards a task, which you learned about as an important influence for or against procrastination in chapter 1. This chapter provides you with insights that increase your expectations and thus your motivation. In order for you to understand these insights, it is a good idea to carry out the corresponding tasks.

First of all, a small warning: The insights are a matter of opinion. You don't have to insist on rediscovering yourself in every insight. It is enough if you agree with the insight, the task helps you and you are motivated to fulfill the otherwise postponed duty. It is quite possible that the realizations are too simplistic for you. Some of the contents in one insight even contradict the contents in another insight from this chapter. But this is not a bad thing. Because the goal of the insights is to give you food for thought. How you use them is entirely up to you.

Insight #1: You'll never regret anything once you get it over with

This realization first encourages you to remember. Think back to the last time you did an important thing that you didn't feel like doing. Try to trace back the emotions and thoughts you had before doing the task. In some circumstances, it will have been acute unwillingness. You may have had low motivation. In addition, there were a thousand other thoughts that distracted you and tempted you to do something else.

But what did you do? You defied those odds and carried out the task. You demonstrated enormous willpower and a strong sense of duty to yourself and possibly even to others.

What was it like during and after performing this task? At first, it might not have been easy to do, but by the middle of the execution, you were in the flow.

Could it even have been easy? It was suddenly actually not so difficult to take on the task and perform it with appropriate quality.

How did you feel after it was done? All the barriers were gone at once: you were relieved, proud, happy; yes, even free!

Next, think of another situation where you did a task that you didn't feel like doing for any reason: What were your emotions before, during, and after doing it? Collect in your memory as many situations as possible in which you successfully beat your inner resistance.

My experience

This realization has helped me massively. For me, it was probably the most effective measure against procrastination. I used to envy people who pursued their private goals in a highly disciplined manner, who turned their hobbies into their profession or consistently followed through with their diet. When, in rare situations, I followed through on otherwise postponed tasks, I noticed how well it made me feel. It was then that I realized that before performing an unwanted task, I might even feel unwillingness for the rest of my life. But one thing was also certain: after performing it, the pride would be all the greater! After forcing myself to perform postponed tasks for one week, I managed to feel this moment again and again, the feeling of pride after the task was completed kept increasing. Eventually I had a smile on my face even before starting to perform the task – today I will successfully prove it to myself again! It became easier for me to motivate myself each time.

With the first realization, you are made aware that overcoming is only temporary. Pride and satisfaction in completing the task, on the other hand, are long-term. Unfortunately, the same is true for the negative: if you decide not to perform your unwanted duty, stress about the pending completion and other negative emotions will also be long-term. To help you understand the simplicity of it, here are some choices for the situation:

1. You have the choice to struggle with yourself and decide against performing the task. The result is that you feel relieved for a short time and pursue a preferred activity. However, you will not develop maximum pleasure in this

preferred activity because you will still be preoccupied in your subconscious mind with the task that needs to be accomplished. If you don't do the task at all, you will be unhappy in the long run.

2. Likewise, you are free to struggle with yourself, to try to perform the task and to stop at the beginning because the task does not suit you. This is, after all, a step in the right direction. Try to take away lessons from the attempt and stick with the task a few minutes longer each time.

3. The third option is that you are aware of the challenge, but think back to the many times you have already overcome and successfully pursued an unloved task. You realize that you will be happy and relieved after completing the task. So, you generously allow plenty of time to complete the task, create the most inviting atmosphere possible for completing it, and persevere with it. In between there are breaks every now and then. Don't let anyone or anything rush you. You struggle with yourself for a brief moment to get over yourself. After that, you complete the task and feel proud over the long run.

Task 1

Imagine the third scenario in relation to the tasks you have been putting off. Sitting down in a quiet environment with your eyes closed, visualize for several minutes how you successfully overcame the resistance, and gratefully receive all the positive emotions after the task is done. The important thing is to feel these emotions properly! Make every effort to feel the freedom and bliss after the performed task. Do this exercise several times a week or several times a day. Don't you want to finally tackle this task; to take the credit and prove to yourself what a strong-willed and consistent person you are? It's all up to you...

The advantage of insight #1 is that it is universal in nature. It is applicable to any type of task and any type of interpersonal relationship. Visualizations, as described in Task 1, are a powerful way to motivate yourself using your imagination. You see yourself at the goal and feel the success before it is achieved. By doing so, you make completing the task more attractive to yourself and increase the benefits you generate from the task.

Insight #2: The goal is progress, not perfection

Perfectionism often masks a fear of not living up to an impression of oneself or one's work. Students often face this problem, according to the *University of North Carolina at Chapel Hill*. Procrastination, which results from striving for perfection, is unfortunately based on the wrong thought processes. For one thing, perfection is not attainable by waiting and procrastinating on one's duty. For another, perfection itself is a term that leaves much room for interpretation and usually describes an impossible goal.

The focus is only on the first aspect, namely the counterproductive waiting time. Obviously, a person has the goal of delivering a perfect performance due to his or her previous performance or for other similar reasons. The delivery of this performance is postponed due to doubts about one's own competence. Think about it logically: you want to deliver perfectly, but you doubt your competence. The only solution in this situation is to acquire the competencies. This only works if you take on the task as soon as possible. The other things you are *always perfect* at, you are doing very well anyway, right? So why do you prefer these *kids' games* to big challenges? Perfection – and this is a segue to interpretive latitude – is hardly admirable if all the time you're only mastering challenges you're comfortable with, isn't it? Prove true perfection to yourself by acquiring new skills and delivering an unexpectedly strong performance!

Now to the second aspect mentioned: the scope of interpretation of the term *perfection*. Perfectionists usually overlook the fact that there is not just one interpretation of perfection. What is perfect for you may not be for other people. Moreover, when you work, study, or otherwise perform in a way that is judged by others, you are subject to the mood swings of those individuals in their evaluation. General perfection does not exist. What is even more striking is the fact that people who are not perfect also enjoy prestige: They have stains on their clean slate, but usually enjoy more admiration than other people who appear perfect. This is because there were obviously obstacles that did not pass by these persons without leaving a trace. But still, these individuals have mastered their way. Isn't that worthy of admiration? Isn't it perfect, in a sense, when a person successfully manages not only the things that are like child's play for him or her, but also the distinct challenges that are noticeable in hindsight?

Task 2

Think about what the term *perfection* means to you. As you do so, think about how weaknesses might play a critical role in the recognition of achievement. Is it possible that you would receive more recognition if you completed a task that everyone knew you were not good at? And wouldn't it be absolutely impressive if you mastered this task with a very positive result?

Changing your attitude is not easy. It is especially difficult if you have only known one view of perfection in your life up to now. But it is worth turning your own way of thinking around. You will discover that perfection – if it exists – does not automatically mean faultlessness. In the end, small mistakes even make you likeable, because they testify to humanity. Mistakes and weaknesses help you to stay grounded. Because if someone takes off, he can lose his perfection by underestimating challenges and making careless mistakes.

Insight #3: Not by hook or by crook, but with breaks and stages.

Behavioral and brain research shows that setting stages is helpful in achieving goals. A stage is an intermediate goal that can be checked off as *done*. The world-renowned behavioral scientist Gerhard Roth has put forward a number of theses regarding habits that can be seamlessly applied to other circumstances. Gerhard Roth cites the division of the major overarching goal into stages as an important step. It is important to make the individual stages more attractive with rewards. The rewards should be varied and beneficial. *Varied* means that the rewards should not lose their attractiveness, and thus their usefulness, at some point because they are used too frequently. *Conducive* provides that the rewards should not conflict with other goals or frustrate progress in performing the task.

Task 3

It is not possible for every task, but if it is feasible in your case, then divide your previously postponed task into several stages. These stages should be such that you feel more motivated to pursue the task. At the same time, the stages should be large enough to make progress. For example, there is no benefit to setting a task for 30 minutes a day if you need 15 minutes to work your way in. So determine meaningful stages. Set rewards for when you reach the stage. Make sure that the duration of the stages gets a little longer each time. This way you will get used to performing the task for a longer period of time.

If you are working on the task for a long period of time, it pays to build breaks into the completion of the task. Working for 2 hours at a stretch is generally not beneficial. Breaks in between are helpful for productivity and to prevent distraction. If you have an impulsive nature with little self-control, as you learned about as a possible cause of procrastination in the first chapter, you will best understand that distraction carries a high risk of stopping task completion. How about allowing yourself this distraction, but only during certain periods of time? Wouldn't this be an excellent compromise, thanks to which you could give in to impulses, but at the same time be highly focused on your duty?

A top technique for balancing work on the unwanted task and breaks is the *Pomodoro Technique*. It works as follows:

1. Formulate task (e.g., your daily stage).
2. Set first work stage and set alarm clock (e.g., 25 minutes).
3. In the time slot consciously pursue only this task.

4. Point out the status of the work and the progress made in carrying out the task. Possibly address a few motivating words to yourself: "I have mastered the first part great!"

5. Take a 5-minute break and set an alarm clock. During this break, it is allowed to give in to distractions or practice other preferred activities.

6. After the break, start again from the beginning.

7. Perform 4 of these time-break blocks and then take longer breaks.

The important element here is the alarm clock. Without the alarm clock you would tend to deviate in time. Through the alarm clock you have a clear signal that immediately calls you to the next step of the Pomodoro Technique.

Insight #4: Start with the most unpleasant task

If you have a choice, it is recommended to start the day with the hardest task. At the beginning of the day, you still have many hours ahead of you. Accordingly, the confidence to successfully master an unpleasant task is greater. In addition, productivity is highest in the morning. Well rested and more in front of you than behind you, the drive tends to be great. The prospect of having completed the unpleasant duty early in the day and then being able to spare the entire day for pleasure usually has an inspiring effect.

Task 4

Try to get at least some of your unpleasant and previously postponed tasks done first. This doesn't necessarily have to be at the beginning of the day, although in terms of productivity it is of course a good idea. Should you be putting off tasks at work and the work doesn't start until 2 p.m., as a rule, of course, you can't do the task in the morning. It's simply a matter of doing the unpleasant duties first at the beginning of each task section. How does that make you feel? Are you inspired, because you have done the most unpleasant things at the beginning and now you have all the freedom for the pleasant things?

You automatically avoid a feeling of pressure and melancholy during the day by doing the task right at the beginning. In addition, concentration is higher in the morning because the body is refreshed after sleep, due to improved release of the sleep hormone melatonin, if it takes place under optimal conditions (room temperature around 18 °C, fresh air, comfortable mattress, darkness, six to eight hours duration). A strengthening breakfast and morning coffee also have a beneficial effect. At breakfast, care should be taken to avoid sweet spreads and other sugary foods. Because yes: sugar is also detrimental to consistent task performance. First, sugar has a stimulating effect by shooting into the blood and providing instant energy. Then the blood sugar level drops rapidly and cravings set in. Nobody wants to start the day like this, let alone carry out unpleasant tasks! So, the ideal cornerstone is to successfully carry out the unpleasant things as quickly as possible with all the fresh energy in order to then make room for the pleasant tasks.

Insight #5: There is no beginning and no end, only doing

Some people approach an unpleasant task with vigor at first. They firmly resolve not to put it off. But then comes the question, "Where do I actually start?" This question often ruins all good intentions. A motivational film inspired by a true story called *The Peaceful Warrior – Path of the Peaceful Warrior* highlights this when the gymnast in the film has everything one could want at his age; until fate takes a turn for the worst... and all the doctors tell him that he will never be able to practice sports again with the knee injury he suffered in his life-threatening motorcycle accident. But he manages to do it thanks to the help of an old man who slowly leads him back to his old strength. The gymnast, when asked by the old man to resume gymnastics, thinks he is completely off his rocker. "But I don't even know where to start!?" He is plagued by fears, doubts, the huge road ahead, the neigh Sayers etc., so that he not only tends to procrastinate, but is completely at a loss as to whether to do it at all. The old man's words are "There is no beginning and no end, only doing."

In his song *Alles was ich hab,* artist Fynn Kliemann encourages people to, "just think about it. Problems become more comfortable later and don't matter afterwards." In this context, it's more about the general attitude to life. In his view, people don't have much time to live and tend to make too little of it. Possibly, many people feel that life is passing them by. Because yes: Procrastination can also take on such characteristics – precious life passes you by and many opportunities are not ceased because too many concerns prevail. It is always postponed!

Use this time to think back to the situations in which a supposedly difficult task became easier the longer you worked at it. There have already been such situations in your life, right? Either the big hoopla was over after only 2 minutes when you realized that it's possible, or you already got used to something after a few weeks or months, so that all the initial difficulties were relieved by the routine. Often the question of the right beginning is related to other problems, like insecurity, striving for perfection, lack of ideas due to a lack of motivation, and so on. In fact, it is confirmed that the longer you pursue something, the simpler it becomes. In this sense, you can have even the worst chaos in front of you, but you will make a good start, as long as you *do* just start. Grab one part of the task and get started! Everything else will come with time. Sure, you will have to rework and correct due to the lack of a plan in the beginning, but this will be easier in the end once you have the full overview of the entire task.

Task 5

Think of at least one of the tasks that you are not at all comfortable with. On a sheet of paper, write down all the subtasks that it involves. Now write down all the points that you have to accomplish in the subtasks, if a further subdivision is possible. At the end, look at your list and mark with a check mark the subtasks that give you an idea of how to get started right away. Maybe you even really feel like doing some of the subtasks? Do this exercise for as many tasks as you can that you would otherwise put off. Each task broken down into subtasks, or other smaller items, will give you more opportunities to find a good starting point.

The exercise is as simple as it is ingenious: On the one hand, you subdivide the task and set milestones. On the other hand, you show yourself the many individual steps. With an overview of the individual steps, you can even work through the subtasks cross-wise without order if that helps you at first. Feel free to start at the end if you like this subtask. It is your free decision. In the course of this subdivision of the often postponed task, you may even find that the task has many aspects in its individual subtasks that you like.

Now to come to the last big trump card of this subdivision strategy: By successfully accomplishing many subtasks, a synergy effect occurs. What does a large whole, such as the task in front of you, consist of? It consists of several individual smaller parts! These parts have to be connected, which requires synergy. Now you are completely on the winning track because the more subtasks you complete, the more the synergies will have their effect. So, you will become better and better able to cope with the whole task. With this in mind, may I once again remind you of Fynn Kliemann's words, "Problems become more comfortable later and don't matter afterwards."

In the same way, later on the tasks become more comfortable for you, until they are unimportant afterwards, because you have all the necessary tricks up your sleeve and the whole task is no longer a problem. But to get this far, you need a smart start. Pick one of the many subtasks and just do it. Everything else will come by itself. Start with the subtask where you make fast progress.

The most important things in a nutshell

> ➢ If you visualize how happy you will be after completing your duty, your motivation will increase. Use your imagination. Focus on the positive emotions you will have after completing the task. Think back to the moments when you were relieved after completing an unpleasant task. **In retrospect, you will always be proud!**

➤ Perfectionism in its official definition of faultlessness and flawlessness is not attainable. Moreover, perfectionism that consists only of meeting easy challenges is less admirable. If instead you set progress as your goal, you will lose fear of the task and expand your competencies.

➤ Difficult tasks are best tackled with a clear plan. If rushed, the risk of poorly performing the task or failing altogether is great. A plan with breaks and stages for completing the task is better.

➤ When the day begins and productivity is at its highest, you ideally start with the unpleasant and deferred duty. Your resources are greatest at the beginning of the day and encourage discipline.

➤ It often turns out that if an unwanted task is done consistently for a while, it's not as hard as you thought after all. That's why it's helpful to start in the first place. If there is no plan yet, just start with the easiest part of the unpleasant task. Once the beginning is done, the more you do it, the more the other problems will fade away.

Concept 2 | Self-efficacy: Conviction of success

This chapter is useful for people who tend to put off tasks due to doubts about their capacity to succeed. You have to work on increasing your self-efficacy. In addition to being useful for people who suffer from generally low self-confidence, this chapter is also great for perfectionists. Those who don't tackle tasks, because they doubt, they can live up to their personal idea of perfection, need more confidence. But a lack of self-efficacy can also occur in even the most confident and competent individuals. Because confident individuals with expertise in the task have little doubt in themselves, the only possible causes of sudden lack of conviction are external, such as an environment that continually emphasizes the negative aspects of an activity. If the devil is painted on the wall, the risk arises that the task which is actually tailor-made will suddenly be postponed due to doubts.

Lack of self-confidence.

Lack of conviction.

Negative environment.

These and other hindrances must be dealt with in order to increase the likelihood of performing a task. However, this chapter is not only about execution. Your goal is to accomplish the task as convincingly as possible. But how is it possible to activate conviction of success and thus high self-efficacy in the face of several negative influences?

The easiest way is to have your own positive experiences. Clearly, if you've already seen that you were capable of something before, you'll have a greater conviction that you can do it again. The more often this happens, the more unshakable your conviction becomes. If you have successfully performed a task hundreds or thousands of times (by the way, these numbers are absolutely realistic with respect to some tasks) then no one will be able to take away your conviction in a hurry. Your belief in success will be huge. Your self-efficacy will eventually be at a high level.

But what happens when one's own experience is lacking? Especially new challenges present uncertainties to people with self-doubt or a negative personal environment. If you have to manage something new or lack positive experiences, then you need methods. This chapter contains 4 methods with corresponding exercises for you to do.

Method #1: Learn from the model

Model learning according to the psychologist Bandura is known under various names: Imitation learning, model learning, observation learning and more. In some cases, distinctions can be made between these terms, but they are not relevant for this guidebook.

In model learning, an existing model is used to learn from. The model does not have to be present. Videos, stories, news articles, newspaper articles and other sources are great for this purpose. You achieve the greatest effectiveness with the best learning process when you watch videos. Because videos show you moving pictures in which you gain processes, positive emotions and numerous other impressions that make it easier for you to become enthusiastic about the model. Model learning can take place in both positive and negative ways. If you look at it in the words of Karl Valentin, "We don't need to educate our children, they imitate everything we do anyway." It is clear that children especially learn through this medium. Copying parents has produced many a child who adopted the same inhibitions for example – this is model learning with a negative effect. Conversely, there were plenty of children who learned their parents' discipline partly through a strict upbringing and partly through their own observations.

Successful model learning works best when the tasks are simple. Learning to skate for example, without hands-on practice is impossible. On the other hand, there are less complex things like hammering nails into the wall and creating an outline for a term paper. All these things can be learned well using a model. It must be ensured that there are recordings of the model. Without video recordings or at least texts model learning it just doesn't work.

The great thing is that you can find plenty of video material to help you learn how to stop procrastination on YouTube – The most popular social network for videos doesn't miss a topic. There are two ways to find the right videos: Either you enter the search term "*stopping procrastination*" or other closely related search terms, or you directly enter the task you want to perform. In connection with this, it is important that you enter this task in such a way that YouTube suggests videos with instructions: So not "*stop early rising*", but rather "*early rising tips*" or "*early rising tutorial*" would be optimal. For some topics you will have to search longer, for others shorter. But you will definitely find models as you try. Also, use the power of feature films and series: If you have a popular series or movie character who can serve as a model against procrastination, watch him/her often!

We learned in the first chapter that lack of conviction about the occurrence of personal success is one of the main causes of procrastination. Perfectionists are also affected by this. This lack of conviction is called low self-efficacy. Self-efficacy can be developed by watching people accomplish a task. This works best when you have a positive or neutral attitude toward the person in question and the person is accomplishing the task under the same or worse conditions than you. An example of this I suppose would be to watch a video on social media of a person doing weight training without hands. So, what excuses are there now for not starting to exercise? Certainly not the excuse that you yourself cannot succeed. A great example that can be useful in any context is Stephen Hawking. Abundant video footage, documentary films, written records and various impressions of people around the world serve as models that show how a person confined to a wheelchair from his young adulthood, and increasingly limited in speech, became one of the most important scientists of our time; as well as rich and famous worldwide. After these examples, what excuse is there for you to put off doing anything at all? Ideally, look for models who start out in the worst possible conditions, but still accomplish the tasks you are resisting.

Phases of model learning

Model learning consists of 4 phases. An important part of it is the reinforcement and motivation processes, both during the execution and/or afterwards. In Bandura's view, learning is not a reaction to the environment (e.g., one observes an event and realizes that one needs to learn about it), but an active process of observation. This means that one observes a particular performance in others and decides to acquire it. Model learning can also be passive, in that observations are made without wanting to learn a thing. Then, a latent knowledge develops anyway; that is, a knowledge that is available but is not called up because one's own readiness for it is lacking. You should not lack readiness, after all it would be better to eliminate the postponement voluntarily and with a willingness to learn.

> ➢ Phase 1 – Acquisition phase: In this phase, you focus closely on the model. What it does, how it does it, and how it motivates itself is carefully observed. The greater your willingness to learn and the stronger your will to stop procrastination, the more attentive you will be.

> ➢ Phase 2 – Retention processes: Store the observed behavior as well as possible in your mind. The more of the behavior you retain and the more it is rooted in your mind, the more likely you are to recall what you have learned.

> ➢ Phase 3 – Reproduction processes: You imitate the behavior. Either you do it for practice or directly in the situation. Based on the retention processes, the behavior of the model is reproduced, whereby even small steps (e.g., the completion of a part of the postponed task) are purposeful.

> ➢ Phase 4 – Execution phase with reinforcement and moti-
> vation processes: Reinforcement and motivation to prac-
> tice what has been learned (e.g., due to motivating words
> from other people or self-praise) creates an incentive to
> implement what has been learned on a regular or sustained
> basis.

Model learning is not the same as finding and observing a role
model. It does include this step, but it consists of several other
points. You notice in every detail that it is a psychological model.
From this type of professional psychological model, you are very
likely to achieve great results. Keep in mind the important points
that model learning teaches you in addition to finding and observing a model: attention, memorization, reinforcement, motivation.
These are all important parts of the big picture.

Task 1

With all the important clues, now for every single task you put
off, find at least one model that does it better. If you only put off
one task, you only need one model. If you have several different
tasks, you will have more work to do because you will have to look
for more models. Watch the model in as many videos as possible.
Make sure it starts in about the exact same condition with the exact same challenges or in worse condition so the observations
catch your attention. Write down all the things the model does
correctly. By writing them down and reading them regularly, you
will better remember the means by which the model, and presum-
ably you, can fight internal resistance. Set small rewards to help
motivate and reinforce the process. Dedicate yourself to working
on the model for each postponed task every day for at least a

week. Learn from the model, implement it, and see how it helps you.

Motivation is the key

Motivation determines whether model learning really moves you forward, or rather falls into the category of *latent knowledge*. Latent knowledge means that you've probably learned something, but it's not completely getting through to you. You lack the incentives to put the knowledge into action. For you, this would mean that the task would remain in procrastination and no improvement would occur. A reason for lack of motivation is given when the model starts under more favorable conditions. Model learning degenerates into a joke when you learn from a model who has mastered a task perfectly anyway. For a person who was in the armed forces for 20 years, had to get up at 5 a.m. every day and do morning sports, getting up early is a cinch. Often the problem with such models is that your inhibitions cannot be understood and the advice has no effect.

> ➤ **Lesson 1 for more motivation on the model**: Great motivation is ensured through identification. The better you can identify with a model, the easier it is for you to develop the motivation to implement what you have learned in the model.

Further information about the model is an influence on motivation that should not be underestimated. If, for example, you find out that the career person you chose as your model achieved all his professional goals, but was lonely and had a failed family life, your conviction and motivation will crumble. Such models are not helpful for model learning, but there is another use for them: Using these models, who subordinated their family life to their career or prioritized it in a different context to the detriment of other desires, you learn better how to decide whether your goals are right: How big is the benefit of the task? Is procrastination appropriate, or logical; should I abandon the task? (See: Chapter 1)

On to the actual text: What should be expressed is the importance of the model's other career. If the model became satisfied by performing the task and had a fulfilling life or a good reward for performing it, you will gain a greater conviction and motivation to do the same.

> **Lesson 2 for more motivation on the model:** Prefer models that, in addition to the successful execution of a duty, have also been able to profit from the execution in the long term. In this way, you will promote the reinforcement process in the execution.

Notice

Model learning can also be done the other way around. By using a model to see how much something is hurting you, you do everything you can to make it better. For example, the children of alcoholics experience it in an extreme way when they suddenly step into their parent's urine on the way to the toilet because the parent *couldn't hit*. Violence as a result of alcohol consumption, accidents and other radical experiences also leave such an impression that the negative model leads to positive behavior. Therefore, in conversations with the children of alcoholics, it can often be seen that they have not touched a drop of alcohol until later adulthood because of the negative model in the parental home. In this sense, it proves to be an interesting approach to choose a negative model. If you're tough, you'll choose an extreme model to show you exactly how serious the situation is. Basically, positive models are more purposeful.

Either radicality works in model learning or it turns into the opposite. Therefore, it is best to always start with models that serve as a moderate example. If these examples do not show any effect, then you can gladly change to a more radical model. Each person is his or her own best teacher. Be brave in exploring the models and discover the right one for you. In the beginning, don't be intimidated by a model that is too strict.

> **Lesson 3 for more motivation from the model:** The discipline, consistency, and other skills that the model teaches you should not be discouraged by the fact that they are difficult for you to implement at first. Choose a model that you can keep up with.

Method #2: Trick your body

Albert Bandura's observation that physiological states are a source of self-efficacy expectancy leads us to the second method. Physiology describes functions and processes in the body. Physiological processes always take place in connection with the expectations of a task. Some are so deeply hidden in the human being that we cannot trick the body when they occur. An example of this is hormone releases that cause us to look at a task with strong dislike or feel stress at the thought of it. As a result, we may put it off. As mentioned, the body cannot be tricked in these situations – or can it?

In this method #2, processes are presented where we *can* trick the body after all. These include increased heart palpitations, tremors, weak knees, sweating (especially wet hands) and similar symptoms that you can feel and identify directly. So Method 2 is about obvious and usually outwardly recognizable signals from your body. Your body gives off these signals in response to something. It is likely that your body is giving off these signals because it is feeling discomfort in thinking about an upcoming unwanted task.

The above examples of physiological states, i.e. increased heart palpitations, etc., you have already experienced in your life in numerous situations. Certainly, these symptoms do not occur only at the thought of an unwanted task. They also manifest when you have something positive coming up. You realize that the same physical processes that occur when you think of an unwanted task can also manifest when you have positive things coming up. And another thing: How many uncertain, difficult or dicey situations in which you had sweaty palms beforehand have ended positively for you in the end?

So, you have at least 2 anchors with the help of which you can trick your body: On the one hand, you can occupy the physiological states with positive emotions based on your positive experiences; on the other hand, you can defuse the physiological states with positive experiences in negative situations. *Anchor* is the keyword here, which leads you directly to practice with another task.

In Neurolinguistic Programming (NLP) there is a method called anchoring. It was created to evoke positive resources in one's own body in negative or difficult situations, virtually at the push of a button. NLP itself is a collection of psychological strategies, methods, and procedures that were assembled in the 1970s by John Grinder and Richard Bandler through observing the most successful psychotherapists. Although some core theses have since been disproved, NLP is used in diverse fields for a wide variety of purposes. Whatever keeps you from performing a task – whether fear, striving for perfection, lack of attractiveness of the task, negative experiences in previous attempts etc. – NLP provides ways and means to overcome the challenge. One of the methods in NLP that can be used most flexibly to solve various problems is anchoring. The basic idea behind anchoring is that whenever you get into the situation where you don't feel like doing the task or are afraid of doing it and are putting it off, you set the anchor to evoke a different mood in you. This is because during your exercises you condition yourself to feel positive by using the anchor.

Task 2

Anchor. Choose the physiological state (trembling, increased palpitations, etc.) that you experience when confronted with the unwanted task. Think of the many instances with positive outcomes where you felt the same physiological state. Close your eyes and think carefully about each situation, focusing on the positive moments. *Feel* those moments. Now comes the important part: set an anchor before this exercise. An anchor should always be unobtrusive. You can discreetly and quietly snap your fingers, tighten your toes or briefly blink your eyes. The important thing is that the anchor does not attract attention. Because that way it can always be used. By setting the anchor you enter into your positive perception of the respective physiological state. Practice this anchor several times a day for a few minutes each time for several weeks.

Practice makes perfect because it produces the intended conditioning. When you get into the habit of thinking positively during each physiological state, an automatism develops in the brain. Automatisms are ingrained in the brain and simplify our daily routines. There are both positive and negative automatisms. A negative automatism is, at the upcoming thought of the task at hand, to hear a palpitation, to get anxious and to postpone the task. A positive automatism is to hear heart palpitations at the arising thought of the upcoming task, to anchor the positive feeling of anticipation based on positive experiences with heart palpitations in your life, to look at the task with more confidence and maybe even to completely accomplish it on the first try.

Finally, it should be noted that you can trick your body with many positive emotions. There is no physiological state that cannot be filled with positive emotions based on your past experiences. Here are some examples:

➢ Sweaty hands: Nervousness before the interview, but where you got the job absolutely convincingly and with ease.

➢ Shiver: Cold during the trip to Antarctica, which is a highlight of your life due to the company of family and/or best friends and many sights you saw.

➢ Weak knees: Insecurity before an important performance in front of an audience, for which there was an incredible amount of praise and admiration afterwards.

These ideas are just to inspire you. You will find plenty of positive emotions in your life that you can anchor. The more successfully you master anchoring, the stronger you will anchor the positive emotions, even in the most difficult situations when the respective physiological state occurs. This will subconsciously increase your expectation towards the task, strengthen your confidence, and thus, contribute to a higher self-efficacy.

Method #3: Let other people convince you

One more Bandura, then it's over. The psychologist cites social persuasion as a source of self-efficacy. According to Bandura, social persuasion leads to more confidence in one's own abilities. Further, the thesis put forth in this guidebook holds true, that contact with fellow human beings is helpful, even when confidence in one's own abilities is present, but drive is lacking. Other people can have a far-reaching effect on your actions.

Sympathies and trust: Did you already experience having sympathy for that one person you wanted to impress at all costs? If you did it wrong you pretended, but at least you overcame your mistake, which led to actions that you would otherwise not have performed. If you did it right, then the person served as an initiator for you to question yourself and get better. People you trust are most likely to have this effect because several years of intense relationship, leads to paying attention to each other's words. Consequently, these types of friends are able to cause great changes for the positive in oneself.

<u>Intelligence:</u> It doesn't always have to be years of relationships. Sometimes just one intelligent person who sounds convincing and argues sensibly is enough to convince you of the need for a change in action. These *bus stop acquaintances*, which sometimes last no longer than 5 minutes, and after which there is never a reunion, can give you numerous insights and make you believe in yourself.

<u>Realism:</u> For persuasion by other people to work, it is also important to be realistic. A person who promises you the blue of heaven is not your key against procrastination. More effective are people who have successfully helped you in life as often as possible. "*Never change a winning team,*" as the saying goes – so why shouldn't it work again with the same person who has helped you get on a successful path before? Above all, seek out contact with people who know how to build you up. A rock in the wall is often your parents, partners or spouses, even children, if they are adult enough. Good friends should not be ignored either.

People with real-life help records who have helped you more than once are a good place to start. Realism and good success rates in previous conversations, gives weight to the words, which is why you will be all the more convinced. It is similar to the existence of something: if the existence is uncertain and no one shows you it, you are unlikely to be convinced of its existence. But if the person puts the thing on the table for you, you will be fully convinced. Think carefully about the people who have always presented your strengths to you in black and white and never let you even begin to doubt them. They motivate you the best.

Success and competence: Success and competence often prove a person right. People who have, themselves, been successful in the matter you are resisting, and/or have competencies to show in this regard, are more credible. If a man stands in front of your door and pretends to be a policeman, would you have him show you his badge, or grant entry at the drop of a hat? Let people show you their "*badge*" so that they can convince you best. Professionals in the subject areas that relate to your deferred task are helpful. Speaking of model learning: Real people from your environment that you can touch and talk to are also models. This is where you are most likely to get individually focused recommendations that will help you overcome your problem. You can hardly find better models!

The point of this third method is to put together an environment that helps you, not one that slows you down. A negative environment is a common cause of procrastination. If all you hear around you is that you shouldn't do something or that you're incapable of doing something, you'll eventually be forced to believe it yourself. You will now learn how to create a conducive environment in 3 simple steps. Keep in mind that a positive environment will help you in all aspects of life and not only in stopping procrastination.

Step 1: What is generally right, what is generally wrong?

Of course, no human being is inherently wrong. Everyone is made up of both positive and negative qualities. Also, people change. So, this first step is not meant to make you accuse or break up with certain people. It is only to point out which person is wrong company for you at a given moment. It is not meant to be disparaging. Imagine, for example, that you and your best friend share a number of common interests. However, your friend knows absolutely nothing about ice hockey and is not interested in it, whereas you are a passionate ice hockey fan and player. Because he is your best friend, he can be moved to visit your games every now and then, even though it wouldn't be a suitable permanent program. But you have other friends who are interested in field hockey. They like to talk about hockey generally, and they also like to watch your games. The bottom line is that we have to admit that your best friend is not the right person to talk to in the context of ice hockey and is not the right company in your hockey related goals. This does not devalue him at all, because after all he is competent in other things and invaluable for your general environment.

And here lies the important point, that you yourself carry a share of responsibility in keeping your environment positive: You cannot expect to receive approval and to enhance your abilities when you talk to others about the wrong things. It is true that you can sound out interests here and there and possibly inspire people to try something new, just as they are probably trying to do with you. But if, after a few attempts, your interests don't align, then it makes no sense in continuing to exchange views. You run the risk that even your best friends and family will not correctly assess your skills if they have no idea about the subject.

Task 3

Think about how it could be if you often seek advice from the wrong people in your circle of acquaintances. In this context, *wrong* means that they are unable to give you appropriate advice due to a lack of experience, lack of expertise, and/or lack of interest in the topic. If this is the case for you, which people should you turn to more regularly that have more expertise in the respective area?

The problem with people who are not knowledgeable in a field is that they will usually give you the wrong advice. Because they don't know the subject well, they may try to play it safe. *Playing it safe* usually means restraint. Restraint, in turn, leads to less activity. Less activity may go hand in hand with procrastination. So your goal in conversations should be to regularly choose topics that match your interviewees' skills and experience over the long term. Then you'll be more likely to get realistic and credible motivation that places your strengths in the right context and moves you forward. So, in general, the right thing to do always involves mutual competencies in the situation at hand.

Step 2: Which people do you need in your environment?

Again, a note at the outset: This step in no way dictates how you should compose your environment. It is not based on any stigmatization or one-sided characterization of people. Every person is more than his 1 or 2 competences. Every person is capable of disappointing even in his or her greatest field of expertise, or of surprising all along the line despite a supposed lack of competence. People's individualism knows hardly any limits, which is why every person in your environment – as well as yourself – deserves to be heard. But one thing cannot be denied: Somewhere in our subconscious, it plays out that some advice from certain people becomes particularly deeply ingrained, while certain advice from other people doesn't even make it into the top 100. The reason for this is that some people have certain qualities or preferences that make them particularly heard. Let's start from your deferred tasks: What you definitely need are people who can help you in terms of procrastination because they bring certain qualities to the table. This doesn't mean (!) that all other people in your environment are unimportant. So, at this point, the case is purely made for expanding your environment, not for shrinking it. Which companions do you need for your "*mission against procrastination*"?

> Connoisseur: This refers to the people who have always succeeded in boosting your confidence. Who has a high level of persuasiveness? Who has almost always been able to inspire you?

> Realists: Realism creates logic. Logic creates conviction. Conviction creates opportunity for success. Chance of success creates self-efficacy. If you have people around you who give you realistic arguments for good chances of success, you will develop more willingness to accomplish the task at hand.

> Experienced: These people have experience with the task you are resisting. They have performed the task themselves or have observed it several times in other people. You are guaranteed helpful tips on how to do it and how to stick with it from the experienced ones.

> Models: Basically, like the experienced ones, only with the advantage that they were in the same, a comparable or an even more adverse situation than you when performing

the task. The degree of identification with these people is high.

➢ Theorist: Unlike the *experienced* and *models*, these people have a theoretical knowledge of the task you are facing. Complications can arise, especially with tasks that have a high practical relevance. A lower credibility towards these people can creep into your own subconscious. Nevertheless, good tips are possible. For tasks with a theoretical reference, the theorists are ideal.

➢ Drill Sergeant: These people do not necessarily have to have theoretical or practical knowledge. They do not have to be experienced or good models in relation to the task. Realism is not necessarily their strong point. And most of the time they don't know you anyway. These are simply people who are highly disciplined in everything they do. Likewise, they always demand the maximum from their environment. They are doers who often lack interpersonal skills. But every now and then, a spark of their almost pathological obsession will jump out at you. Important: Too much companionship to these individuals can be counterproductive. At worst, it will cause you to overexert yourself. So, it's best to use drill sergeants when you're at risk of backsliding after initial consistency. Ideally, they will give you a powerful push in the right direction.

Task 4

You don't have to have each of these or similar types of people in your environment. It is enough if 3 of these types are present and have a certain effect on you. Try to find out how often you need contact with these people and which of these types of people are most important to you. Then it is likely that you will find the support you were hoping for in these people, who will put you in a positive mood and convince you of your qualities – or drill you from time to time so that you can convince yourself of your qualities.

Step 3: Negative environment – does such a thing even exist?

In the first step, we found out that it is partly due to your perceptions and decisions whether an environment is negative. By choosing the right topics, you can let the people around you give you a positive feeling and in turn motivate other people in the best possible way. The latter is also important, after all, relationships are based on mutual added value and mutual sympathy: not only should you be motivated, but you should also motivate others.

Another part of whether an environment is negative or not, however, is far beyond your control. There are people who primarily look negatively at things. For some, this almost degenerates into a disease: Almost everywhere disadvantages are seen, pessimism outshines any other thoughts. Sometimes the pessimism in these people is temporary, because they are going through a bad phase. If they are good friends, people important to you or good people in general, it is important not to turn away from them. Stand by them and be their pastor as long as it does not burden you. Because only if you help other people in their predicaments, can you expect the same from them. Especially if you know the negative thinkers from their positive side as well, it is worthwhile to remain loyal to these contacts and help them back on the right track. If you notice that negative thinking is affecting you too much, then the time is ripe to step back for a while. That being said, and this is not meant to sound macabre, these individuals lend themselves to negative model learning. You see how bad negative thinking can be, and you do better yourself. Even if their negative thoughts have nothing to do with your deferred duty, they can encourage you to pull yourself together in order to approach life more positively yourself.

Task 5

Do good, and good will happen to you! Look for people in your environment who are important to you or have helped you several times, but are currently in a bad shape. Stand by these people regularly for a while. Try to motivate each other. If you don't get any motivation, don't worry. After all, you are doing an important person a favor, which will improve the mood around you. Eventually, it will pay off.

But what about people who have been thinking negatively for years or decades and have made it their main task to consistently complain about life? If it is true that there are such people in your environment, then you should carefully consider whether the relationship in this form still makes sense. If these people are important to you, then try to help them. But their attitude must change. Because thinking only negatively for years or decades is not a strategy for life. These people are not suitable for negative model learning, because they could harm you. Especially in the case of people to whom you do not have a strong connection, it is advisable to break off contact as quickly as possible if only negative things are permanently conveyed.

Why does this guidebook advise these radical upheavals? Apart from the fact that you may have had to experience how stressful it is to deal with their problems and negative beliefs, there is a scientifically proven risk of contagion. The keyword here is the so-called mirror neurons in our brain. When in the frequent company of people who think negatively, we can unintentionally adapt their way of thinking.

My experience

Here I can report from the other perspective. I was not negatively influenced by merciless pessimists but was rather myself the merciless pessimist who negatively influenced the people around me. For a long time I did not understand this. So when, conspicuously, many people from my circle of friends stopped contacting me, I was astonished. Only over time, as I transformed myself into an optimist through reading books about success and increasing my own success, did I understand what a burden I must have been to other people. So, I know first-hand that pessimists are not beneficial to your environment.

The most important things in a nutshell

- ➤ A strong sense of self-efficacy gives you conviction, and confidence in your abilities. You can best strengthen your self-efficacy by learning from the model, tricking your body and a positive social environment.
- ➤ Learning from a model is nothing more than learning from role models. These role models can come from reading or video material or be people in your environment.

The important thing is that they are in a situation that is as comparable as possible to yours.

➤ You trick your body, by using anchoring techniques to change its negative reactions to the postponed task, with positive emotions, and memories. "*My heart was pounding so hard the last time I lifted the trophy at the Junior Championships and celebrated the greatest success of my youth!*" Program this mindset firmly into your thoughts through exercise, and more positive associations are likely to precede the un-wanted task, encouraging you to perform it.

➤ An all-positive or all-negative environment does not exist. No person is simply bad or good. You should judge things depending on specific situations and topics of conversation. In connection with your task, set up an environment that encourages you.

Concept 3 | Self-control: Defying and focusing on impulses

Self-control can be defined in many ways. People are in control when they don't immediately flare up when someone criticizes them or upsets them in some way. When it comes to performing tasks, those who do not allow themselves to be distracted are considered to have good self-control or to be disciplined.

Discipline, self-control related to performing tasks, and self-control related to reactions are all about resisting emotions. External stimulus lead to emotional reactions, which are either automated, mentally controlled or a mixture of both. The goal of this chapter is to help you control your emotions. Longing to give in to distraction, aversion to the task, anger at a person who stands in the way of completing the task – all of these should become a thing of the past.

But how do you switch off or reduce your own emotions when humans are emotional beings? Brain research shows that the limbic system reacts first to external stimuli. Emotions form in the limbic system in the neocortex. This means that, no matter what we think, emotions always come first. Only subsequent activity in other regions of the brain makes it possible for us to weigh our actions.

Since you can't turn off your emotions, control becomes even more important. This chapter shows you how to create automatisms that will slow down the emotional effect when a negative impulse occurs. In the long term, this approach will help you to act and react in a more controlled, deliberate and goal-oriented manner, not only with regard to procrastination, but also to life in general.

Before you work on the long-term aspects of self-control in Step 3 of this chapter, you'll get some short-term *first aid* in the first 2 steps. These short-term steps, combined with long-term practice, will help you gain more over all self-control.

Step #1: Ideal conditions as a basis

Depending on which task you want to pursue, there are specific ideal conditions. Tasks that are theoretical in nature for example take place in a quiet environment which helps with concentration – less distraction means fewer impulses. Fewer impulses makes for easier self-control. But not all tasks take place in a quiet environment. For example, sports at the gym, where the environment tends to be noisy. Or family obligations where small children are present. Again, it can get noisy and hectic. A person who has little ability to cope with the high activity level of children will tend to react impulsively in one way or another.

Now ask yourself what is more likely: that you will learn to control the impulses, which are firmly anchored in your character, through methods, *or* that you will have greater self-control by creating ideal conditions that counteract impulses? The answer is more likely the latter. The reason for this is that in the first scenario, you have to fight against a part of your character, whereas in the second scenario you are simply preventing it from being triggered.

Think of it like a protective wall that wouldn't be able to withstand an onslaught, so you build an additional wall to reinforce it. Or maybe you know people who are sensitive to certain issues. It is just smarter not to bring up the subject that triggers them rather than triggering them and then trying to deal with their emotions. Another example, specifically related to procrastination. You know that the ringtone on your smartphone is preventing you from completing a task, so you simply turn off the smartphone.

To build a protective wall against impulses and potential distractions, you must first identify the attackers. Only by precisely naming them can you plan countermeasures. First, choose an ideal place. Taking into account the aesthetics. For example, if unwashed dishes dominate the landscape, this will have a distracting effect. Order and aesthetics are important in helping you combat procrastination, so choose a place that you find visually appealing. Also check if you feel comfortable in your seat, notice if smells are pleasing to you and so on. Listen to sounds; in sports for example, it could be that the music played at the gym doesn't appeal to you, but maybe you can bring your own headphones. When reading, quiet music is more conducive. Every person is different, some don't like studying in libraries or at home because it's too quiet for them. They prefer busier places where things are happening. How you get into your flow is up to you. Just make sure you're in a place that doesn't make you put off the task due to

unwanted music, an uncomfortable seat, or other such factors –
conjure up a place that you really like.

Conclusion: Choose a place that ideally combines suitability
for the task and your well-being. By choosing an appropriate
place, you do not even have to identify the triggers of procrastination in the first step, because the probability of their occurrence
is reduced by your choice.

My experience

How individual each person is evident in my preferences:
When I sit at home in silence and comfort, I can hardly focus. I
prefer to work in places where there is movement. Cafés are ideal
for me. I also enjoy working in the waiting area of the gym from
time to time. Basically, I have no problems with noise at work.
When something is going on, it increases my creativity. So have
the courage to choose your place with a certain stubbornness and
really listen to what helps you perform the task; even if it seems
absurd to others.

Step #2: Identify triggers for procrastination and determine countermeasures

Here we focus on the small triggers that could occur despite
having chosen the optimal place to do the task in. Digital devices
play a big role in distracting us. The problem is that they have
become a habit. Even when we set the goal of not using them
while performing our task, reaching for the smartphone is automatic. It is the automatisms that take hold.

Other smaller triggers to consider besides digital devices are dietary related. For example, people who use sweets as a kind of *compensation*, but end up with belly aches and downers, or certain people in the environment can be distracting, like work colleagues who pull you away from a task all the time.

Conclusion: Triggers exist that are location-independent. Smartphones are the most common example. People can also take on the role of negative impulses, discouraging you from completing a task and causing procrastination. Spotting these subtle triggers helps determine countermeasures.

Task 1

Now it's time to practice. First, establish one or more environments that make you feel good and are conducive to focus. Then visualize what specific triggers might occur. Write down these triggers so that you can determine countermeasures for each one as you go along.

Now you'll learn how to determine countermeasures. What if you need the procrastination trigger to perform the task? This is exactly the problem with digital devices. Smartphone or laptop, which bring multiple distraction factors through popping messages, calls, media offers and other functions, are usually needed at work. The key question in finding a good solution here is what options are available to limit the range of functions or add features that mitigate the trigger characteristics. An example on the smartphone: WhatsApp is your temptation, but the smartphone is needed for the activity. How do you reconcile doing the activity on the smartphone with resisting the WhatsApp trigger? One solution is available in the smartphone itself, namely to turn off the ringtone. If this is not enough and the brightening screen distracts you when you receive messages, then you can disable the message notification so that the screen does not brighten. Nothing will happen until you check WhatsApp yourself. Also, programs or add-ons with features that minimize distractions can be downloaded for free or purchased for a small price.

Did you know?

There are special apps on the market that can help you with procrastination. They are either programmed with a focus on specific tasks or can be configured individually. *YellingMom* is one example. The app starts making noises as soon as you don't follow up on your task at the required time. The apps usually create impulses through a high "annoyance factor" that obliges you to perform the task.

The case where the source of negative impulses is at the same time necessary for work does not only apply to digital devices. People can also be a similar problem. You may have that one person in your environment who always has a way of keeping you from completing a task. Again, we come to the topic of negative and positive environment, which we already had: You were told why you should create a positive environment and how to do it. Let's say you can't avoid the disruptive person because they are necessary to perform the task. Such scenarios occur especially when good and bad students are put together in group work. In our example, the bad students distract the good ones. Simply excluding them is not an option. Similar cases can occur for adults. A solution is difficult to find. Radical countermeasures would be to blackmail or force a person to cooperate and stop interfering with the task. Less radical, but uncertain in terms of effectiveness, would be telling the teacher.

Countermeasures for triggers: Not always an easy thing to do that sometimes requires resourcefulness. The more important the task, the less scruples you should show. After all, being blocked from succeeding by a preventable negative influence is incredibly annoying.

Here is an overview of a few possible triggers of negative impulses and countermeasures that minimize the susceptibility to procrastination:

Disruptive factors	Countermeasures
• Loud music • Noise • Distraction through negative words	• Earplugs • Headphones and instrumental music
• People	• Spatial separation
• Animals • Insects	• Protective sprays • Spatial separation • Procurement of external assistance
• Bad odors • Tempting smells (e.g., sweets)	• Change of location • Nose clip • Remedy the cause • Airing

Task 2

As a continuation of Task 1, let's determine countermeasures for your personal triggers. Feel free to use the ideas from the table and previous text and add to them. In the end, you should have a sheet of paper on which your ideal measures are written, which you can use when you are confronted with your negative impulses.

Step #3: Develop long-term self-control

Steps 1 and 2 serve as short-term and situational measures for more self-control. Because this guide is intended to help you as quickly as possible, but the character traits are not quickly changeable, you have first dealt with the external measures. Now you come to the inner measures; that is, what happens inside you and occupies your thoughts when an impulse affects you. If you get the impulses under control like this, you don't even need the first 2 steps.

Now for the procedure, so that you can work on yourself in the best possible way:

➢ If you can already control yourself for a short moment without immediately giving in to an impulse. Start at the subchapter titled "*Third*".

➢ If you start the task and do it for at least a short time until you postpone it, even though you don't feel like it. In this case you overcome the impulse for a while. Start at the subchapter titled "*Fourth*".

➢ If you immediately give in without thinking about it or making an effort to suppress the impulse. Start at subchapter titled "*First*" right at the beginning.

No matter where you place yourself above, start at the recommended step and practice all the steps up to the fifth, and it will help you to develop long-term self-control. The advantage of long-term self-control is that you minimize or even eliminate the effect triggers have on you so that you will rely less on the short-term actions from the first two steps in this chapter. This reduces the overall effort required of you.

First, become aware

In order to work on the solution to a problem, you must first become aware of the problem. When you consider how many people carry around heavy stuff in their subconscious, it becomes clear that not every personal problem is known to the person concerned. Dishonesty towards oneself can be observed quite often. Hiding a problem start with a lie. As an example, we can mention an overweight person who keeps postponing her diet or gives in to the first impulses after a few days: She has heard that there are people who are overweight because of a disease. Since then, she persuades other people that this is the case with her. Others develop understanding and no longer judge her because of her weight. So, she feels secure with her excuse and eventually begins to believe it herself; not necessarily literally, but in a modified form, considering herself not responsible for her weight. This occurs with procrastination as well. If tasks are put off out of fear, but the person does not want to admit his fear, he might find other reasons for putting them off.

Becoming aware of your problems serves as an initiator for long-term changes by ensuring that no further negative impulses develop.

The best way to raise awareness is to look inside, while at the same time asking others how they assess your reasons for procrastinating. Remember the tips on creating a positive environment from the last chapter? The more of the recommended character types you have in your environment, the better they will contribute to a complete picture of your character. A realist who has been friends with you for many years will not mince words in naming the problems clearly. Ask them to give you their honest opinion without shying away from your reaction. Write down the problems that people see with you without judgment.

The other reliable method for identifying your problems is to search within yourself. Nowadays, people hear so much from friends, from superiors, in the media, from newspapers etc. etc. it is really beneficial to simply deal with ourselves more often. All of your unique truths lie within. Becoming *aware* of them is a long process.

The following task will help you even if you think you are aware of all your problems. It is not uncommon for people to live what they think is an ideal life, but there is something inside them that is oppressive. Feel free to use this task on a regular basis in order to be "up to date" with your mental state even after you have eliminated your procrastination.

Task 3

It will be difficult to get into the habit but do it at all costs – journal for at least 15 minutes every night. You don't have to write for the entire time, but you should at least spend that time thinking and getting something down on paper. Some days there will be more writing, others less. That's normal. What do you think about and *how* do you think? Think in a quiet environment and don't let anything distract you that would cloud your concentration. An ideal place is an armchair at the table. You can also lie down on your bed and write while lying down.

Write down in your diary with regards to your day: 1. what happened, 2. what you thought and felt about it, and 3. what caused your feelings in the described situation(s). All 3 steps are necessary, because if you only write down what happened, but don't include your emotions, you will have a log, but not a helpful diary. Keep a diary for 2 weeks before taking stock of whether you are more aware of your problems. Then continue with the exercise for as long as necessary.

You will gain important insights through this inner dialogue as you practice every evening. Be careful that you don't invent "substitute impulses" for putting off the task. In the long run, you will not be able to hide from yourself or lie. You will become aware of your problems and be able to deal with them head on.

Second, use beliefs.

Beliefs are statements that you anchor deeply in your subconscious through repetition. It takes time for their effect to strengthen. It's all a matter of how quickly your brain develops the automatism to cultivate a different thought when confronted with the impulse. In the case of beliefs, you replace a previously negative impulse that encouraged you to abandon the task with a positive impulse that encourages you to get going and keep at it.

Let's first shed some light on what the subconscious is. To this end, think about processes that you know well. Whether it's cooking the same dish, driving a car, or doing your job – there are things you do well even without thinking. The reason that everything works automatically are automatisms. Science has located automatisms partly in the subconscious. Partly, because some scientists deny the existence of a subconscious. If by the term sub-conscious we mean a place in the brain, the deniers are correct. But if we think of the subconscious as a collection of automated processes and thoughts, as defined, for example, by the science site *Spektrum,* then the deniers are wrong.

The first person who dealt with the subconscious and called it "the unconscious" was Sigmund Freund. His trains of thought are still taken up today and reinterpreted again and again. Today, the unconscious mind stands for all thoughts, feelings, processes, and other things that occur in our brains without thoughtful ef-fort. If you think about how strongly some behavioral tendencies are noticeable in some people, there must be a reason for it, right?

> ➤ If a person always reacts aggressively, it is in his nature.
> ➤ If a person always expresses pessimism, it is in his nature.
> ➤ If a person is incredibly disciplined, it is in his nature.

But these characteristics are not innate. Individuals either ac-quire them or choose not to. Model learning, which we have talked about, is one reason why people acquire certain behaviors. But behavior can also be acquired through persuasion. If a person has doubts about themselves because of negative experiences and keeps mentally repeating to themselves, "I'm a loser. I'm a loser." the probability increases that this depressing and discouraging thought will become firmly programmed in the subconscious.

Now the connection of all this with procrastination: if a neg-ative reaction to an impulse is firmly anchored in you, which pre-vents you from performing a task, then reprogramming the subconscious is a key to solving the problem. This is nothing more than taking steps to help you replace existing automatisms in your brain with others. So, if up to now, when you had an impulse, you thought of abandoning the task, now you develop an opposite belief set, such as: "I am staying on the task because the task offers me... (name benefit)."

Task 4

Develop beliefs that make the stimulus unattractive. One or two sentences per belief should be enough. Important rule: do not use negations (e.g., not, none) because the subconscious mind does not perceive them. Clearly state the attractiveness of the task and make the stimulus unattractive. Repeat your belief regularly. It's best to say it in front of a mirror for 5 minutes every morning.

Automatisms are therefore the goal; beliefs are the way to get there. If you practice automatisms by saying beliefs out loud with focus and conviction, you will be better able to resist the initial temptation. After several days or a few weeks of practice, you should be able to suppress, at least temporarily, the impulse that tempts you to procrastinate. This will be the key to a little more self-control, because your first thought from then on will be, "Wait, this impulse is unattractive because the task gives me advantage XY." So, the first resistance is stirring, which is a start on the path to self-control.

Third, set stages, carry out increases

If you are able to defy the negative impulse for a while and perform the task, it is a success. Congratulations on that! Now you will work on increasing the amount of time you defy the impulse. This action helps to toughen you up. If you defy the impulse a little longer each time and do your task, you will be better able to resist the impulse in the long run. Self and impulse control are often mentioned in the same breath as self-discipline. This is because increasing discipline means being able to resist negative impulses more effectively over a longer period of time.

Now let's get practical: You increase your self-control by proceeding in stages. You set a stage up to which you want to persevere without giving in. Then you give in to the impulse. After giving in, you decide whether to resume the task or abandon it completely. Because it depends on the type of task, there are no guidelines here.

Some more information about the stage: If you manage to hold out until the stage you have determined, then a goal has been reached for the time being. After that, you move on to the next goal, namely a longer stage. In order not to overexert yourself, it makes sense to maintain a stage and to reach it a certain number of times.

Let's assume, for example, that you are dissuaded from your plan to drink less alcohol and study in the evening instead, because you are tempted by student life: Stage 1 could be to drink only on the weekends, if you have been doing it more often. After you've managed this for a month, drink only on a weekend day. After this has worked for two months, you increase the stage again to a level you want. The point is to keep increasing the requirements until you reach the level you are aiming for.

Task 5

Determine which stages are realistic and sustainable for you. Consider at what intervals you feel comfortable increasing the demands. Choose a pace that suits you and is encouraging.

You make each stage more attractive to you and increase your discipline when you set rewards. These rewards are given to you whenever you have done everything according to the plan. The rewards, however, should not be allowed to undo your progress. Everything should be coordinated in such a way that it moves you forward.

Another way to increase your discipline is to keep a record of your progress so that you can visualize it or write it down. For this purpose, you can use your diary from the first step. If you have decided to keep a diary for the long term, you will now benefit twice. As you can see from keeping a diary and recording your progress, all the steps in this book are interrelated and have the greatest effect when they are carried out together – ideally in the prescribed order. An alternative to the diary for documenting progress are checklists, visualizations with pictures, and conversations with other people in which you report on your progress. Here you include the environment as an important factor already presented.

Fourth, find the release valve for the pulse

The fourth point of your self-control cure pulls the pin on the effectiveness of the impulse. You have already learned to control the impulse for a time while performing your task. However, one problem that is likely to remain, is that as the task progresses, it continues to push you to give in to the impulse. The trigger of the impulse to procrastinate has its effectiveness: after spending some time on the task, you notice that you feel drawn to give in to the impulse. The initial belief that the impulse is unattractive weakens with the duration of the exercise, because it can no longer be denied that you actually don't want to do the task.

At this point, it is important that you stick with the first 3 steps presented in this chapter and do them regularly. Continue to practice the pronunciation of the beliefs every morning. But how do you manage to improve the effectiveness of your beliefs so that you consistently stick to your task and the impulse no longer feels so strong? The solution is a release valve: for every impulse there is at least one appropriate release valve, which has the advantage of reducing the effectiveness of the impulse because the impulse has already been yielded to by the release valve. An example from anger therapy is sport: the anger impulse is weaker if intensive sport has already been done the day before, because less energy is available. This insight is now to be applied to the procrastination impulses. Subsequently, the determination to perform the task is greater.

Task 6

Consider what valves might be useful for your case. Since release valves can vary widely, the frequency and duration of their use required may vary too. Do you need to use it for over an hour every day, or several times a week for 10 minutes each time? For 2 weeks, try out the release valves that come to mind and see how they best help you release your impulse so that you feel as little urge as possible to give in to the impulse during the task.

Exercise and diligence play a role in the release valves. Impulses that show up as too much energy (e.g., aggression, impatience, restlessness) are usually remedied by exercise. If you have exercised yourself physically and/or mentally properly, your urge to indulge will be less – after all, where is the energy supposed to come from?

Other impulses (e.g., doubts, discouragement) may occur during the course of the exercise when you realize that it is not going according to plan. In this case, it is worthwhile to use a tip from the previous chapters as a release valve: start with the easier part of the postponed task. Then you will see that you are capable of accomplishing the task. Your doubts will be removed.

If you tend to get distracted by electronic devices, the best way to counteract the impulse is to set aside time slots during the day when you allow yourself to use the devices with full abandon. But beyond that, use them only when necessary. In this way, you have used the impulse itself as a release valve, only at a more appropriate time.

Fifth, transfer positive trends

Once you've gotten to the point where you've increased the stages and reduced the effectiveness of the stimulus through dump valves, there are only 2 steps left for you to slowly but surely gain long-term self-control.

1. Keep the program from the first 4 steps: In a sense, what you have done so far in the 4 steps is an adjustment. Adjustments and withdrawals take time. When you think

you're out of the woods, the opposite may be true. In particular, changes made too quickly carry the risk of lack of strength. Therefore, maintain the previous program from steps 1 to 4. If you feel that you have had or are having severe problems, keep the first 4 steps for 6 months. If you have a mild case of procrastination, 3 months should be sufficient.

2. In addition, it is important that you transfer the positive trends. Transferring them means that you will also benefit from them in other areas of your life. Because the more situations you demonstrate self-control in, the more it becomes a new defining character trait. If it comes to the fact that you have changed your character fundamentally to a controlled one, then you do not have to follow the first steps anymore and radiate full control in any situation – an absolute character gain!

Let's assume that you would radiate self-control only with regard to the postponed task: true, this would correspond to your goal of being able to perform the task better without giving attention to the interfering impulses. But if self-control were lacking in all other areas of life, you would be at risk of relapsing. Because at some point you would no longer practice the first 4 steps (journaling, etc.) consistently, and gaps would gradually appear; gaps in which your previous character traits might show through. If, on the other hand, you completely change your character and transfer the self-control you have gained to as many areas of your life as possible, you will expand your new automatisms. The brain gets used to reacting in a controlled manner in more and more situations and to weighing up whether the respective impulses are worth it before giving in. Think about it: In which situation is it not advantageous to weigh things up before making a decision? Only in a few exceptional cases. So make it your trait to be able to defy impulses and temptations in order to be more successful everywhere in life, to stop giving in and to stick to your own goals and dreams.

How do you transfer the positive trends into other areas of your life?

1. Do all the exercises from First to Fourth for other areas of your life! When journaling, stop focusing only on how you deal with and feel about procrastination, and start focusing on other tasks, challenges, and joys of the day. Proceed in this way for all 4 of the previous steps.

2. Start with the simplest challenges! If you want to make your character more controlled beyond procrastination, you should develop goal-oriented beliefs to solve all problems. Preferably start with the items where you find it easier to exercise self-control.

3. Let yourself be tested! If possible, regularly put yourself in situations where your self-control is put to the test. This also means hard cases. Character is defined primarily by behavior in extreme situations; surely you remember the *Teachable Moments* from the introduction to this thesis... Make sure that you have absolute control and that even stronger impulses do not throw you off balance.

The most important things in a nutshell

- ➤ Before you train your character to be more self-controlled (long-term measures), you provide the ideal conditions to get immediate help against the negative impulses (short-term measures).
- ➤ Ideal conditions are created by a work location that offers as few distractions as possible. You should also identify the impulses and determine countermeasures that you will play out as soon as the impulses occur.
- ➤ In parallel, you begin to work on making self-control your trait in the long run.
  - o To do this, first keep a diary to become aware of all negative impulses and the effect on your emotions.
  - o Formulate and regularly repeat beliefs that are the first automatism to help you not immediately give in to the impulse.
  - o Set stages to stay on task longer and longer without procrastination. Increase the stages over time.
  - o Find release valves for the emotions that arouse the negative impulses in you, to rob the impulses of their effectiveness.
  - o Transfer the benefits of acquired self-control to other areas of life to make self-control your new general trait, which becomes instant and automatic in all contexts.

Concept 4 | Prioritize, relax and decelerate

It is conceivable that you postpone 1 or more tasks because of too many duties. For this reason, it is important to show you another point of view. This view sees the fault not in you, but as a classic phenomenon of today. In this increasingly digitalized and fast-paced world, it can be hard to say "*no*" to the many prospects that present themselves. If you want to take advantage of all the opportunities that come your way as quickly as possible, you may be overextending yourself. Even the most disciplined and competent person would develop a long-term urge to procrastinate in this case.

This chapter provides guidance to help you determine if you have too many burdens. If so, it provides you with ways, means, and guidance to help you better prioritize. You will learn the importance of free spaces, which are a great benefit to your health. With free spaces you will be able relax and decelerate from this digital fast-paced world, in order to recharge your energy. Because one thing is clear: without replenished energy stores, you'll be putting things off more often anyway. A person is only human – an often-forgotten fact in a digitized world.

The more you practice and the better you manage to switch to relaxation mode even in high-stress situations, the busier your schedule will be able to be without having negative effects on your psyche and health. As you can see, if you do everything right, a large amount of duties and tasks is not necessarily bad. But step by step...

Science with a clear opinion

Thanks to the fact that digitization is on everyone's lips as is progresses, it is being well researched. With the effect on the psyche increasingly coming to the fore. *Springer Professional* quoted the following statement by Miriam Goos from the book *CSR and Digitization*:

> *"The digital age has a major impact on the perception and importance of health in humans. Mental illnesses caused by sensory overload of the brain and by the rapid changes of the digital and globalized world are clearly on the rise in recent years."*

Depending on the company, up to 40 digital programs may be used on their work devices. In addition, areas are being digitized that were not previously. For older workers, but equally younger ones with little inclination for digital applications, new challenges are arising all the time. Companies boast about Big Data and a large variety of professional tools, while workers face higher demands as a result. And while the latest technologies such as Artificial Intelligence promise to simplify everyday life for employees, in most cases the time gained is not given to workers.

Digitization – caught between obligations and perspectives?

But digitization doesn't only have negative aspects that over-burden people. It also provides plenty of new opportunities. At which other point in history has it been possible to start your own business without even renting a store or paying for employees, but rather with just a website and some computer programs? The pro-spects are even more far-reaching. The economy is on an expan-sion course and digitization is playing a significant role in this, as technology stocks are shooting through the roof. Even companies outside the technology sector can develop business models that are easier to expand and market, thanks to digitization. All of these circumstances mean that more opportunities are open to more groups of people. These opportunities even make themselves felt at an early age, when children can better connect with friends through digital devices like social media. Even young people have the prospect of gaining notoriety and reach through digital means.

All these many opportunities for people of all ages are initially something positive. Because perspectives mean freedom of choice. Freedom of choice means a greater chance to live the life one desires. Pursuing one's desires means striving for happiness. Are these conclusions correct? Partly …

After all, access to many options leads to people being spoiled for choice. And because many things can be done at the same time in a digitalized world, people try to *do* many things at the same time. Yet each additional thing on the daily agenda can be over-whelming and lead to procrastination. With that, the core of the problem is clear and a possible cause for your procrastination comes to light: overemployment. Remember how you learned in the first chapter that procrastination can sometimes be the logical consequence of being overwhelmed and doesn't necessarily have anything to do with personal weakness at all? This is precisely the problem that is becoming increasingly prevalent in the digital age.

In addition to the high pressure that people are already under at work, due to constantly renewed work processes, there are also self-imposed challenges outside of the workplace. All of which adds up until at some point the mind no longer work and people procrastinate.

So, the trick is, in order not to lose oneself in the digitalized world, to choose the *right level* of activity and the *right* activities. The way to do this is through prioritization and the incorporation of breaks into your daily life.

Consequences of technostress

Technostress is a term introduced by psychologist Craig Brod in 1984. It describes the modern illness of not being able to deal correctly with ICT (information and communication technologies). Technological, cognitive and social overload due to ICT thus lead to technostress in affected individuals.

Causes of technostress include multitasking (multiple tasks at the same time), the need to be constantly available, blurring boundaries between work and private life, and being overwhelmed by the complexity of technology. The consequences of technostress are sometimes:

> ➤ Exhaustion
> ➤ Headache
> ➤ Concentration problems
> ➤ Burn-out
> ➤ Anxiety

Are not all these at the same time factors that promote procrastination? Certainly, they are!

Burnout often remains undetected in individuals for a long time. The persons wonder why they feel such a strong lack of drive. They are there, but feel mentally absent. Long periods of sleep and a lack of willpower to complete tasks steal precious time.

Notice

Burnout is one of the worst and most powerful causes of procrastination because it is a mental illness. If you have the symptoms of burnout around the clock and very pronounced, it is only right that you decelerate and go to a specialist. He will determine the reasons for your exhaustion and listlessness. Maybe it's not so bad and you only have a vitamin deficiency, but maybe it's depression.

Whenever the world no longer seems bright and motivating, but rather becomes dark and depressing, especially outside of your duties when performing your favorite activities, going to the doctor is the right thing to do.

The other problems mentioned in the list also raise awareness of how many disadvantages result from being overtaxed with digital technologies, preventing perseverance in our tasks. Despite all of this, there are certain competencies that allow people to cope better with it, one such being a high level of self-efficacy. Author Srivastava (2015) cites this as a criterion for coping better with technostress. A high level of self-efficacy is therefore not only helpful in avoiding procrastination, but also in reducing technostress.

So, if you follow all the advice in this book, you'll kill several birds with one stone. Greater self-efficacy reduces technostress, because you accomplish your tasks better and more effectively. Faster task completion, in turn, means you'll procrastinate less and experience less stress.

Step 1: Priorities come before deceleration

Before you actively contribute to deceleration, you should define your priorities. By setting priorities, you end up with a skillfully crafted task list. Then, wherever there are gaps, you have the essential free space for deceleration. How much free space you need is up to you. Most of the time, it's just a matter of trial and error. You test measures for deceleration and see which work best and when.

Getting priorities right requires answers to several questions:

1. What do you need to live?
2. What do you want in life beyond that?
3. How much freedom do you need?
4. What can/do you do without?
5. How do you decelerate and how does it work?

Question 1: What do you need to live?

First, make a list of things you need to live. Normally, the first things that come to mind are housing, money, food and oxygen. All of which are necessary. Apart from oxygen, everything normally requires money, whether it be a purchased or rented property to live in, electricity, water, or food. And you usually earn money by working.

As long as the money you earn is enough, enter only your job in the list. If you have been having money problems for a long time, you should write that you need your job and also another job *or a* higher salary — after all, you have money problems, and they don't go away by themselves. This is equivalent to the first priority you set for yourself.

Deep needs must also be considered. Companionship, friendship and support would be such needs. Only if you believe that you could live your whole life without family, friendship, companionship, and any kind of support, may you omit these things from the list. And if this is impossible, you should write them down.

Task 1

Proceed as described so far, writing down all the things you need on a piece of paper. Afterwards, check your list to see how the things are related. For example, work gives me money and a place to live, so work comes first and you can cross out the money and the place to live. In this way you shorten the list and have the primary things on it.

Question 2: What do you want beyond that in life?

Life also includes wishes, dreams, goals and other personal desires. It cannot be ruled out that there are people who are perfectly happy with what they already have. Individuals who have a job they love, and their family as a balance are sometimes already satisfied. Again, individuals exist who want to have more. In this regard, you should question yourself.

Do not deceive yourself when you answer this question. As you have already learned, human beings have a lot of potential for self-deception. That's why it's important to keep a diary, even for setting priorities. You keep track of, what otherwise, gets lost in the hustle and bustle of the day. Keeping a diary, combined with open dialogue with other people, will help you uncover what you really want in life. Even in a perfect marriage, the urge for variety can still be an important element for your future. Even in a perfect job, there may be a feeling inside that you want to achieve more, which isn't necessarily possible with your current employer.

What you really want in your life beyond fulfilling your existential needs is an important key to happiness. There is room here for dreams, self-realization, family happiness, the little kitschy moments of life, the "*thrill*", closeness to nature, the desire to travel. Your existential needs (answers to question 1) in combination with your desires and goals (answers to this question 2) define how much freedom you need.

Question 3: How much freedom do you need?

If one were to formulate in a mathematical formula how questions 1 to 3 are related, the formula would be as follows:

$Day\ (24\ hours)$
$= daily\ time\ spent\ for\ existential\ needs\ (x)$
$+ daily\ time\ spent\ for\ goals\ and\ desires\ (y)$
$+ daily\ time\ spent\ on\ freetime\ (z)$

So, you have a period of time (x) in which you pursue the activities that fulfill your existential needs. Then there is a period of time (y) that you spend on activities that are related to your desires and goals. Lastly, there would be a period of time (z) that you need for free time. A free time activity that every person needs time for is sleeping. Winged sayings like "You can sleep when you're dead." are sporadically admired by some people, but are by no means sustainable as a philosophy of life. It has been proven that lack of sleep can lead to cardiovascular disease and other serious health ailments. With this in mind, getting enough sleep is a serious matter. Adults are generally advised to get 6 to 8 hours of sleep per day. Follow this advice and you'll be doing your health a lot of good.

"But with 6 to 8 hours of sleep, that's already a third or a quarter of the day sacrificed for free space!" That may be so. But it is this generous period of time for sleep – as defined by nature – that makes it especially clear how important free time is. When it comes to free time, always plan generously. Because once you've accepted binding duties and tasks, it's not always easy to regain that time again later.

Task 2

As a continuation of Task 1, determine in your list the answers to Question 2 from the previous subchapter and Question 3 from this subchapter. Take into account your existential needs and the amount of time required to meet them from the first question. Since all 3 questions are closely related, you should complete the tasks simultaneously. Be honest with yourself. If you notice that the *formula* isn't working because you are imposing too many duties on yourself at once and have hardly any free time, this indicates that your procrastination is the result of excessive demand, rather than weakness of character, lack of discipline, or any other possible causes.

Question 4: What can you do without?

Are there too many tasks on your list and is there too little free time? This is the case if you don't have an hour or 2 during the day to sit back and just laze around. By the way, hobbies like sports don't count as free time if they are associated with pressure to perform. Hobbies must be things that you can enjoy doing leisurely in real free time. Of course, sometimes in life there can be little or no free space for a few weeks, or on certain days. But it must not be all the time, these periods of life should end with a nice break

During free time you shouldn't let yourself be distracted by digital devices. Free time that you spend typing messages, video chatting, or on social media will drain you. Your free time should be like a vacuum that you can use for relaxing activities that spontaneously come to mind.

If there is too little, or too much free time, make adjustments. You may have heard stories of top managers who had plenty of money and suddenly quit their jobs completely because they were dissatisfied with their personal lives. They had been deprived of so much, that in one fell swoop they had nothing, but free time left. This is not a balanced way to approach it. It is far better to work with small, simple adjustments to achieve a better work/life balance, such as:

> Watch less TV in the evening
> Consume less digital media
> Reduce time for social contacts
> Reduce your workload
> Work on fewer desires and goals at the same time (realize one first, then start on the other)
> Get up earlier in the morning (if sleeping beyond 6 to 8 hours)

Task 3

And what about you, what can you do without? Things from this list, or do you have other ideas to add? For your personal situation, write down at least 5 customized items with which you can create more free space.

Question 5: How do you decelerate?

After you have created the rooms, you should occupy them. How you occupy the spaces you made will be revealed to you in the next 2 steps of this chapter after you have completed question 5. We will discover several interesting methods, ranging from Far Eastern concepts to conventional European medicine.

But before we get to this step, it's worth noting that you should regularly evaluate the measures you are implementing: Have you gained more free time? Do you feel greater urge to perform tasks due to increased relaxation time and effectively recharged energy reserves? If this is the case, then everything is going according to plan. Maybe you even have too many free time now. You could consider reducing it slightly to see if you increase productivity and success in other areas.

What to do if you realize that your free time isn't enough, but you can't create more? In this case, we propose 2 useful solutions:

1. **Get help**. Create "assistance" for yourself. Either literally or figuratively. Literally, means hiring an assistant for example. People in positions of high responsibility are often reluctant to relinquish responsibility. They don't want to leave the well-being of their company, child or any other important things in their lives, in other people's hands. Yet there are plenty of examples where delegation was successful. If you choose people well, you have much less to worry about. Figurative assistance could be for example if cooking takes up too much of your time, you could arrange for other people in the household to take over one dish a day. Or you could order food every other day and save yourself time that way.

2. **Increase quality**. By increasing the quality of your free time, you improve its effectiveness. It's no secret that some people can only relax in certain situations. So don't expect all the exercises in the following steps to work for you. Just test what works.

My experience

A clear prioritization plan, similar to the one described here, helped me to realize that I had a combination of several causes for my procrastination. I had a hard time motivating myself and occasionally got distracted by impulses because I had imposed too many duties on myself. In some ways, it was obvious that there were too many duties. But I always said yes because I wanted to prove something to myself, which I still can't understand today. But now I know that it pays to think first and say yes later. These days, besides work, I have a personal project and a hobby too. I enjoy having time for socializing, cooking, and doing nothing too. These are all valuable components of life in my eyes, that I couldn't do without.

Step 2: Simple introduction to deceleration

You probably know a few simple ways to slow yourself down. Lazing around probably being the best example. However, lazing around only works as a method of deceleration as long as nothing is truthfully being done. Anyone who is lazing around, but at the same time is thinking oppressive thoughts is not decelerating at all. In fact, you would be under mental strain that can cause stress and anxiety on a subtle level. If you are thinking about the worries of the day or you are annoyed that a task has been postponed again, then you are not decelerating at all. Fortunately, there are methods that assist you in focusing properly on the moment.

Method 1: "Slow" trends for individual areas of life

The following "slow" trends will help you to properly decelerate. They are possibly inspired by Far Eastern philosophies but have their origin in Europe where they are on their way to becoming well established. One particularly well-known method is *slow food*.

Slow food stands in direct contrast to fast food. Unhealthy fast foods, that many people reach for when they need something in a hurry, are avoided. No time to eat? That's hardly conceivable for followers of slow food. The movement, which began in Italy in the 1980s, believes that enjoyment should be the focus. Enjoyment can only be guaranteed through quality, and quality entails a certain amount of effort and time in the production process. Ecological and regional dishes are in the foreground here. Taste is not invariably defined as a question of subjective taste, but rather, among other things, as a sociocultural issue that should be debated. In the eyes of the representatives of slow food, the trend toward fast food is because more and more people are losing attention to food and no longer taste it properly.

If you have an affinity for delicious food, you may find slow food an excellent option for deceleration. Here is a suggestion for the evening:

➢ Turn off the TV
➢ If you have a partner, cook together. Otherwise cook alone
➢ Make the evening an hour shorter without TV, but spend it together, talking, laughing and reminiscing with home-cooked food and a glass of red wine instead

Whether alone, with friends at a barbecue, or visiting a restaurant, slow food and slow cooking is a sensual way to relax, which can become a great hobby.

Another interesting trend is slow travel. With slow travel, you avoid hotels, airplanes, luxury events and the like, which are usually associated with the perception of deadlines, waiting times and large crowds. Instead, you opt for a form of vacation where you travel with little means. As a result, you're usually close to nature and local people, which at the same time, offers you more authentic insights into your destination. Considering that traveling and vacations are usually meant for recreation, but stress often becomes a big part of it, slow travel seems to be a good solution. If you have noticed so far in your exercises that vacations did not bring the desired relaxation, Slow Travel is made for you!

Feel free to read up on other slow trends on your own. The Internet will provide you with plenty of inspiration. If you want, you can even develop your own slow trends. If it works for you, just give it a try. Theoretically, if you have a lawn that helps you to relax and "let your soul dangle", there's nothing stopping you from "slow mowing" even.

Method 2: Sports, music, art – but without pressure to perform!

Earlier it was mentioned that sport only serves to slow down as long as it is not linked to performance pressure. Because having fun is an important factor in distracting yourself from the thoughts and worries of the day. The same applies to other forms of hobbies, like music or art for example.

If these activities are linked to performance pressure, they should be classified with your goals and desires instead of hobbies and free time, because it is not casual deceleration. This differentiation is important. You should internalize it so that you don't do sports for 5 hours a day and wonder why you still don't manage to relax.

Here are some examples to illustrate the point:

➤ You play soccer in a club. The training times are prescribed, you have to win the games. You have to worry about offside traps and tactical triangles.

➤ You play the piano. Soon you'll be performing at a concert. There are several concerts like this every year, and you always prepare meticulously for them. Performing in front of large crowds makes you uncomfortable.

➤ With your craft skills, you have the goal of being accepted into a gifted course to develop with others at your level. Although only a hobby, you must meet requirements for admission and perform well to remain part of the course after admission.

How are you supposed to be able to relax in these scenarios? The stress of work and everyday life is now followed by the stress of the hobby. If you were doing it just for you, it would be different. But under the pressure of having to deliver and meet standards, the activities are demanding.

When sports, music or art is really practiced for relaxation purposes, without performance pressure, then positive effects on the psyche are medically well documented.

A study by Sandra Klaperski and Reinhard Fuchs of the Albert Ludwigs University in Freiburg, using 149 inactive male test subjects, found that lower cortisol levels (cortisol is a stress hormone) and a reduced heart rate were the benefits related to regularly practicing sports.

Scientists from Taiwan studied the benefits of yoga in stress management. People were divided into groups so that one group practiced yoga and another control group remained inactive. The group with yoga practice showed a decrease in stress levels and improved autonomic nervous system function after 6 to 12 weeks.

If at this point you start to lose the connection to procrastination, consider the path you have taken in this step: You have decided for yourself that you procrastinate because you have too many obligations and too little free time. As a result, you have decided to build free time into your daily life for relaxation, and deceleration, as well as to improve your mental state. If you improve your condition, you will be able to perform your duties and tasks much better. So, the mental improvements from exercise are likely to give you an "anti-procrastination kick."

Did you know?

It has long been known that sport acts as a "panacea". An article in *SPIEGEL* tells the story of Joanna Zybon, a running therapist who works in a Berlin correctional facility. She helps those with problems ranging from drug withdrawal to depression to sleep disorders. Sport is used as a multifunctional means of thought therapy. Even to the point where it can have an anxiety-relieving effect.

So there's no doubt that sports are a great way to relax and fill in the gaps in your free time. But can the same findings be applied to music and art? In answer to this question, the *SAGE Institute for Mindfulness and Health,* Berlin, compiled findings on the effect of music from several studies with the following benefits noted:

➢ Influencing brain processes and functions

➢ Influencing breathing, blood pressure, body tension and heart rate

➢ Classical music pieces contribute to calm and relaxation, while favorite music promotes arousal

➢ Reduction of stress when listening to relaxation music (lower cortisol levels in the blood)

➢ Positive effects occur sporadically also with physical complaints when music is listened to

➢ Reduction of depression possible

When you play music, the effects are very likely to increase because you are no longer just listening, but completely immersed. You either have to consider certain breathing techniques while playing or concentrate on the music more closely than when just listening. Also, provided you have a good command of the particular instrument, you can release your emotions through it.

The practical thing about music is that you can combine it with other activities. Listening to music while participating in sports or art is something many people do. Which type of music isn't that important at first, but calm, classical music can add a certain neutrality factor. At once offering a calming effect, while not stimulating personal memories. If you were to listen to the song *Unchained Melody* and think of Patrick Swayze and Demi Moore making pottery in the classic movie *Ghost,* for example, there would be a distraction. This is not the case with classical music. You can even listen to this music excellently while performing the task that you usually put off. You may find the task easier then.

Method 3: Far Eastern approaches at a glance

What the Far East teaches has absolutely nothing to do with esotericism. Occasionally, the breathing exercises, meditations and mindfulness exercises are done an injustice by being pigeonholed in this way. People who are not very well informed subsequently doubt their effectiveness. But did you know that numerous Far Eastern methods for relaxation have been reviewed in studies and found to be effective? In the meantime, even European orthodox medicine is opening up to Far Eastern theories.

To prove the benefit of breathing exercises with an example: The *Munich Breathing Therapy Working Group* conducted a pilot project with patients in 2011. Professional breathing therapists did regular breathing exercises with their patients over a certain period of time. The patients' condition improved in terms of clearer psyche, increased sense of satisfaction and decreased anxiety.

Breathing exercises lead to relaxation. Various breathing techniques can be rehearsed, or breathing can be used to support meditation. In meditation, the goal is to focus on the moment. People who have difficulties with this and whose thoughts regularly wander off in the direction of the problems of everyday life can find success by concentrating on their breathing. This is because it creates an anchor that distracts them from their thoughts. Through consistent regular practice, meditation will work better over time, so that the breathing exercises can eventually be omitted.

Task 4

Speaking of the breathing exercises-meditation combo: practice it. Meet this method of relaxation with an open mind. We are not talking about esotericism, but exercises with proven effectiveness. Take a daily window of 10 to 15 minutes to meditate. Sit comfortably in a quiet place. Set an alarm so you don't need to look at the clock and get distracted. Then breathe slowly and concentrate on each breath.

Incidentally, energy drinks and caffeine tablets should rarely be used! Now and then it's okay, but in the context of procrastination, they are counterproductive. They get you so worked up that you tend to stick to the distraction rather than the task at hand. A round of meditation, on the other hand, often provides a focus that lasts for several hours afterwards. So, it makes sense to do the meditation immediately before the task you're putting off, or as close to it as possible. Then your focus is sharpened for the execution without the need for energy drinks.

Qigong, Tai-Chi and Shiatsu are also great relaxation exercise, that have become part of the official relaxation and activity programs in the executive suites of several large companies, as reported by *WirtschaftsWoche*. If you're open to these techniques, check out the numerous videos available on YouTube. Find one that you're comfortable with and try it.

Step 3: Permanently establish mindfulness and deceleration

This third step is the supreme discipline. If you master this step, you will be able to keep your mental and physical condition at a good level, even without much free time and with countless duties being accomplished. Of course, you can't do it completely without free time, but you learn to make the most of even the shortest spontaneous breaks.

First, imagine a fairly busy schedule, so full that you have to rush from one appointment to the next. In between, you only have a few minutes free. By establishing mindfulness on a permanent basis, you gain the ability to slow down even in those few minutes. This is not as easy as you might think. Because between two appointments, your thoughts are usually already on the next appointment. Psychiatrist Michael Huppertz sees a big problem here: *"People are always rushing into the future in their thoughts so as not to miss anything. In the process, they miss out on exactly what is really happening right then."*

What if you could at least overcome the tendency to rush? What if you could create distance whenever you wanted to? This would mean that in the 5 minutes between one appointment and the next, you would have no stressful thoughts. You would rather just be in the here and now, relaxing in the midst of the action.

Like much of what you have learned in the previous chapters, lasting mindfulness and relaxation is a long-term practice.

Task 5

The methods from step 2 have helped you learn to *shut down* at specific times. Now it's time to use your favorite techniques to learn to shut down at any time. Get into the habit of always making good use of the small breaks that occur between appointments or tasks. Here are a few examples:

➢ When you eat, eat slowly

➢ When you're not doing anything, breathe consciously

➢ If you're waiting, practice relaxation exercises while you wait

➢ If you relax with music, always have your headphones and a small music player with you. The older Shuffle ipods are great for this because they don't have functions (e.g. Email, SMS) that distract you

The more often you get used to filling the small vacuum in your daily routine with relaxation and focusing on the moment, the better you will succeed. It's all a matter of practice! As time goes on, you should be able to focus on the moment and fill every moment of the day with mindfulness even without the exercises. One useful method is to always pay attention to the little things that surround you. Waiting outside a building can be excellent to link with being close to nature by looking at the green spaces. Or you can simply pay close attention to passersby and how they go about their lives. To conclude, in the words of an actor in the movie *The Peaceful Warrior – Path of the Peaceful Warrior,* "There's always something going on." Every moment offers abundant wonder. You just have to pay attention to it. This provides relaxation and space, even during small windows of time. Allowing subsequent task to be approached with renewed energy.

The most important things in a nutshell

➢ Scientists, psychologists, psychotherapists and professional associations agree that digitalization is creating new opportunities, as well as new challenges. Among the challenges is a new form of stress, called *technostress.*

➤ Too many options exist, which makes it difficult to set priorities. In work, private life and leisure, this can lead to indecisiveness.

➤ Start to determine whether your procrastination is not a logical consequence of being overwhelmed by too many duties. Reduce the duties where possible to create free space for relaxation and deceleration.

➤ Integrate relaxation exercises into your everyday life. Reduce stress by purposefully decelerating with slowing down processes, such as slow food and slow cooking.

➤ Try to use relaxation exercises and other methods that you have practiced for stress reduction, even in random moments of everyday. If you manage to pay attention to your breathing in the waiting room between your work appointment and your doctor's appointment and concentrate your thoughts solely on the moment, you can end up always being relaxed!

Closing words

If this guidebook has taught you one thing, hopefully it is a fair amount of respect for procrastination. It has the potential to take on morbid proportions. It may spread unnoticed like an ulcer and gradually take over several areas of your life. If you take procrastination seriously as a problem, you have the potential for far-reaching improvement. This improvement will save you from chronic dissatisfaction, lack of success, and possibly even mental illness.

At the beginning, as with a doctor's examination and diagnosis, apply the methods in this book and try to find the causes. Then you can initiate the right "*therapy*" with the respective concepts that are right for you. Then the therapy becomes much more than that. Because the more things you implement from this book, the more you learn to set priorities, reduce stress, gain greater self-confidence, optimize your social environment and generally make the right decisions in life.

Probably the most amazing lesson from this book, which you may even have already found yourself, is to be able to say *no* to a task. In this sense, it's not completely far-fetched that procrastination is not your real problem. Possibly the problem is that you're not completely eliminating the task from your agenda. That's a great lesson for you as you continue on your journey.

Learn to relax, let go, and slow down. By and large, people today, enjoy many options that didn't exist but a few decades ago, due to modern economic and technological advancements. Which is great as it creates more opportunities for you to live the life you dream of. Test these options out! And after you have tested, make a decision about what you need in life, what you want beyond your existential needs, and how much freedom is necessary for your physical as well as mental health.

Set an agenda that is realistic and that makes you want to live life and do the tasks that come with it. Then the likelihood that you will postpone things will decrease. If you do find yourself putting things off, you know what you need to do: either the cause lies within you, which you discover through honest inner dialogue, or it is happening because you have imposed too many tasks on yourself. Apply the appropriate measures with the help of this guide: If you are honest with yourself, then sooner or later you will always find the right solution to lead you to your goal.

I wish you good luck and much success with it!

List of sources

Achtnich, Leonie (2012), Prokrastination: Zehn Tipps zum An-fangen, in ZEIT Campus Nr. 4/2012 von https://www.zeit.de/campus/2012/04/prokrastination-tipps

Ammerlande, Andrea (2019), Beschäftigte leiden unter digitalem Stress, von https://www.springerprofessional.de/ge-sundheitspraevention/stressmanagement/deutsche-er-werbstaetige-plagt-digitaler-stress/16282378

Bühring, Petra (2010), Psychische Erkrankungen: Dramatische Zunahme – Kein Konzept, von https://www.aerzte-blatt.de/archiv/78018/Psychische-Erkrankungen-Dra-matische-Zunahme-kein-Konzept

Canfield, J.; Hansen, M. V.; Hewitt, L.: The Power of Focus – So erreichen Sie Ihre persönlichen, finanziellen und berufli-chen Ziele. München: Redline Verlag, 2013. 1. Auflage.

Dr. med. Nonnenbacher (2019), Großhirnrinde, in MedLexi.de, von https://medlexi.de/Gro%C3%9Fhirnrinde

Eultgen, Simon (o.D.): Pomodoro Technik, effektives lernen leicht gemacht, von https://www.fernstudium-check.de/ratgeber/pomodoro-technik-effektives-lernen-leicht-gemacht

Gimpel, Lanzl, Manner-Romberg, Nüske (2018), Digitaler Stress in Deutschland – Eine Befragung, von Erwerbstätigen zu

Belastung und Beanspruchung durch Arbeit mit digitalen Technologien von https://www.boeckler.de/pdf/p_fofoe_WP_101_2018.pdf

Hauschild, J (2013), Beobachten, fühlen, entschuldigen, in Spiegel Psychologie, von https://www.spiegel.de/gesundheit/psychologie/achtsamkeit-kleine-schritte-zur-entschleunigung-a-890285.html

Jakob, N.& Dämon K. (2017), Was Kampfkunst über das Führen lehrt, von https://www.wiwo.de/erfolg/management/management-auch-fernoestliche-entspannungstechniken-helfen/19553278-2.html

Klaperski S. & Fuchs R. (2013), Effekte eines 12-wöchigen Sport- oder Entspannungsprogramms auf subjektive und physiologische Stressreaktionen, von https://www.sportwissenschaft.de/fileadmin/pdf/tagungen2013/2013_Klaperski_Effekte12Sport-Entspannungsprogamm.pdf

Kucklick, Christopher (o.D.), „Es gibt keinen Hinweis, dass ein Unterbewusstsein existiert", von https://www.geo.de/wissen/gesundheit/22098-rtkl-psychologie-es-gibt-keinen-hinweis-dass-ein-unterbewusstsein-existiert

Leadership insiders (2019), Technostress – eine Schattenseite der Digitalisierung?, von https://www.leadership-insiders.de/technostress-eine-schattenseite-der-digitalisierung/

Lern-Psychologie.de (o.D.), Soziale Lerntheorie: Lernen am Modell nach Albert Bandura von http://www.lern-psychologie.de/skripte/modelllernen.pdf

Leubner D. & Hinterberger T. (2017), Reviewing the Effectiveness of Music Interventions in Treating Depression, von https://www.ncbi.nlm.nih.gov/pmc/articles/PMC5500733/

Lexikon der Biologie (1999), Unterbewusstsein, von https://www.spektrum.de/lexikon/biologie/unterbewusstsein/68591

Lin, Huang, Shiu, Yeh (2015), Effects of Yoga on Stress, Stress Adaption, and Heart Rate Variability Among Mental Health Professionals--A Randomized Controlled Trial, von https://pubmed.ncbi.nlm.nih.gov/26220020/

Mende, Annette (2017), Placebo Effekt: Wirkung ohne Wirkstoff von https://www.pharmazeutische-zeitung.de/ausgabe-462017/placebo-effekt-wirkung-ohne-wirkstoff/

Moestl, B.: Shaolin – Du musst nicht kämpfen, um zu siegen!. München: Knaur Verlag, 2008.

Nier, Hedda (2019), Erhöht digitaler Stress das Krankheitsrisiko?, von https://de.statista.com/infografik/19229/digitaler-stress-im-job-erhoeht-krankheitsrisiko/

PsyGA (2018): Die psychische Gesundheit in Zahlen, von https://www.psyga.info/psychische-gesundheit/daten-,

abgerufen: 23.2.2021 fakten#:~:text=Psychische%20Er-
krankungen%20nehmen%20in%20ihrer,Pro-
zent%20(%20BKK%20Gesundheitsreport%202018)

SAGE Institut für Achtsamkeit und Gesundheit Berlin (o.D.),
Die Wirkung von Musik auf Mensch und Gesundheit,
von https://www.sage-institut.de/wirkung-musik-ge-
sundheit/

Stangl, W. (2021). Stichwort: *Selbstwirksamkeit*. Online Lexikon
für Psychologie und Pädagogik. https://lexi-
kon.stangl.eu/1535/selbstwirksamkeit-selbstwirksam-
keitserwartung/

Stangl, Werner (o.D.), Lernen am Modell – Albert Bandura von
https://arbeitsblaetter.stangl-taller.at/LERNEN/Mo-
delllernen.shtml

Statista Research Department (2013): „Verteilung der AU-Tage
aufgrund psychischer und Verhaltensstörungen (F00-
F99) in Deutschland nach ausgewählten Diagnosegrup-
pen im Jahr 2013" von https://de.statista.com/statis-
tik/daten/studie/189551/umfrage/krankenhaustage-
aufgrund-psychischer-stoerungen-nach-diagnoseunter-
gruppen/

Statista Research Department (2019): „Statistiken zu psychischen
Erkrankungen" von https://de.statista.com/the-
men/1318/psychische-erkrankungen/

Steel, Dr. P.: The Procrastination Equation: How to Stop Putting Things Off and Start Getting Stuff Done. Toronto:
Random House Canada, 2012.

Stollreiter, M.: Schluss mit dem Aufschieben – Endlich anfangen zu leben. München: mvgVerlag, 2014.

Thakkar, N. (2009). Why procrastinate: an investigation of the root causes behind procrastination.

University of North Carolina at Chapel Hill (o.D.), Procrastination gefunden unter https://writingcenter.unc.edu/tips-and-tools/procrastination/

Von der Tann, Marie (2017), Wie Sport der Psyche hilft, in Spiegel Psychologie, von https://www.spiegel.de/gesundheit/psychologie/sport-gegen-stress-wie-bewegung-der-psyche-hilft-a-1173661.html

Zeug, Katrin (2013): Mach es anders!, in ZEIT Wissen Nr. 2/2013

Printed in Great Britain
by Amazon